AUTARCHIES

ALSO AVAILABLE FROM BLOOMSBURY

On Resistance, Howard Caygill
Anatomy of Failure, Oliver Feltham
Conceptions of Liberty in Political Philosophy
Modernism, Leigh Wilson

AUTARCHIES

The Invention of Selfishness

DAVID ASHFORD

Bloomsbury Academic
An imprint of Bloomsbury Publishing Plc

B L O O M S B U R Y
LONDON · OXFORD · NEW YORK · NEW DELHI · SYDNEY

Bloomsbury Academic
An imprint of Bloomsbury Publishing Plc

50 Bedford Square   1385 Broadway
London   New York
WC1B 3DP   NY 10018
UK   USA

www.bloomsbury.com

**BLOOMSBURY and the Diana logo are trademarks of Bloomsbury
Publishing Plc**

First published 2017

© David Ashford, 2017

Materials subsequently incorporated into chapters three and four have appeared
in *Modernism/Modernity* (Winter 2014) and *The Journal of Wyndham Lewis
Studies* (Winter 2014). My thanks to the editors for permission to reproduce this
work here.

British Library Cataloguing-in-Publication Data
A catalogue record for this book is available from the British Library.

ISBN: HB: 978-1-4742-9769-1
          PB: 978-1-4742-9770-7
          ePDF: 978-1-4742-9768-4
          ePub: 978-1-4742-9771-4

Library of Congress Cataloging-in-Publication Data
A catalog record for this book is available from the Library of Congress.

Typeset by Integra Software Services Pvt. Ltd.
Printed and bound in Great Britain

It is the wisdom of rats, that will be sure
to leave a house, somewhat before it fall.

— FRANCIS BACON, ESSAYS (1625)

CONTENTS

PREFACE

'THE WISDOM OF RATS'

*A brief introduction to the Modernism
of self-interest*

'You've seen horrible things, an army of nightmare creatures',
Sigourney Weaver intones. 'But they are nothing compared to
what came before...what lies below.' In offbeat horror-comedy
The Cabin in the Woods (2012), Drew Goddard and Joss Whedon
present cinemagoers with a twist on the staples of the Hollywood
horror movie: these turning out to be nothing less than a formal
system of ritual sacrifice, a perpetual offering of teenage blood
in a series of recurring scenarios, in order to keep an infinitely
greater evil at bay. 'It's our task to placate the Ancient Ones, as
it's yours to be offered up to them', explains Weaver. 'Forgive us
and let us get it over with.' But on being confronted with a choice
between either dying for humanity or else dying with humanity,
the teenage survivors (of a clichéd Redneck-Zombie-Torture-
Family flick) choose to effect one final, quite astounding twist.
Refusing to sacrifice themselves (or rather their last few minutes)
for some so-called greater good, they argue that a civilization
sustained by a sacrificial system is not worth saving. So they opt
for the 'agonising death of every human soul on the planet'. Thus
provoked from their slumber, a primordial race of Giant Evil Gods

rises up out of the earth, in the final seconds of the movie, to bring about the long-averted cataclysm and the End of Mankind.

As surprising as so comprehensive a conclusion must seem the logic behind this rejection of a Categorical Imperative is in keeping with the aesthetic that pervades the whole: an elaborate pastiche of every style in the horror genre, this masterpiece of irony also exhibits that thorough suspicion of institutional power often taken to be a defining characteristic of post-modernist thinking, its rejection of every metanarrative, of every totalitarian system of thought. (In fact, Goddard has indicated that his sinister facility is modelled on his hometown Los Alamos, New Mexico – 'where all anyone does for a living is make weapons for the government'.[1]) Regarded as an expression of the great late-twentieth-century paradigm shift (of what Frederic Jameson once termed 'the cultural logic of Late Capitalism'[2]), the conclusion to Goddard's movie must merit serious attention. For as this new post-Kantian morality attains increasing prominence in Western culture we can surely expect many more stories to end like this. If 'we' are a collective hallucination, count on no one dying to save us.

Perhaps the best-known and most forthright expression of this new individualist morality is to be found in writing by popular novelist and philosopher Ayn Rand. In her novels *We the Living* (1936), *Anthem* (1938), *The Fountainhead* (1943) and *Atlas Shrugged* (1957), and essay collections *For the New Intellectual* (1961) and *The Virtue of Selfishness* (1964), Rand developed a comprehensive and consistent philosophy which rejects any system of ethics based upon altruism – that is, 'not the life of man, not the life of an individual, but the life of a disembodied entity, the collective, which in relation to every individual consists of everybody except himself'.[3] According to

Rand, such systems are merely reiterations of a Christian faith based upon sacrifice – simply substituting Society for God. 'In content, they are merely variants of altruism, the ethical theory which regards man as a sacrificial animal, which hold that man has no right to exist for his own sake, that service to others is the only justification of his existence, and that self-sacrifice is his highest moral duty, virtue and value.'[4] In their place, Rand proposes we install her new egoist and objectivist approach to morality: which 'means that one must never sacrifice one's convictions to the opinions or wishes of others (... the virtue of Integrity) – [and] that one must never attempt to fake reality in any manner (... the virtue of Honesty).'[5] But, 'above all', concludes Rand, 'it means one's rejection of the role of a sacrificial animal, the rejection of... self-immolation as a moral virtue or duty'.[6]

Rand thought of her philosophy as a reiteration of the Anglo-American Liberal tradition: and is in fact often taken to be expressing a quintessentially American rugged individualism. There is good reason for this. For instance, Rand's refusal to recognize the necessity of sacrifice had already been anticipated by Victorian Libertarian thinker and Conservative MP Auberon Herbert. According to Herbert, there never was invented a more specious and misleading phrase than the good of the greater number. 'The Devil was in his most subtle and ingenious mood when he slipped this phrase into the brains of men', he writes.

> It assumes that there are two opposed "goods", and that the one good is to be sacrificed to the other good – but in the first place this is not true, for Liberty is the one good, open to all, and requiring no sacrifice of others; and secondly this false opposition (where no real opposition exists) of two different goods means perpetual war

between men – the larger number being for ever incited to trample on the smaller number.[7]

But Herbert held such a scenario to be 'utterly false in its essentials', a dilemma faked up by those with an interest in promoting the 'mere paganism of numbers', in ensuring that people believe that 'whatever the larger number choose to do is by that very fact made right'.[8] In contrast, Rand is willing to concede that such a terrible choice might present itself in reality, and the moral dilemma dismissed by Herbert is the premise for her novel *Atlas Shrugged* (1957); in which the most powerful people in America decide, one by one, to withdraw their consent and support from the United States, refusing to sacrifice more of their time or talent on maintaining the ungrateful parasites that make up the bulk of the American population, although they know that millions will die of criminal violence and starvation as a direct result.[9] Flying off to their 'Utopia of Greed' in the Rockies, her band of egoists look down upon the last convulsions of Western civilization: 'the lights of the cars were darting through the streets, like animals trapped in a maze, frantically seeking an exit, the bridges were jammed with cars, the approaches to the bridges were veins of massed headlights, glittering bottlenecks stopping all motion, and the desperate screaming of sirens reached faintly to the height of the plane'. In one of the famous, haunting images that close the novel, suddenly the lights go out all over the East Coast; and 'with the abruptness of a shudder, as if the ground had parted to engulf it, the city [New York] disappeared from the face of the earth'.[10]

This apparent willingness to countenance Armageddon in order to prove a moral point suggests there is something new here that is entirely alien to the Liberal political tradition derived from John Locke, upon which the British and American constitutions are based – a fanatical intensity, a logical rigour or consistency, an intransigence that must render utterly impossible the spirit of compromise upon which the Lockean balance of powers is premised – a fact Rand herself recognized. In the final pages of her *Atlas Shrugged* we see one character engaged in erasing the 'contradictions' in the US Constitution (and adding a new clause to its pages, 'Congress shall make no law abridging the freedom of production and trade').[11] And yet the philosophy of Ayn Rand has had a role equal to, or greater than, that of even Milton Friedman or F.A. Hayek in shaping our contemporary neoliberal consensus, having had an acknowledged impact on the architects of Reagonomics such as Alan Greenspan, the director of the World Bank, a series of presidential contenders, and the new breed of American industrialists, who have developed revolutionary information technologies in Silicon Valley. Given the consequences that are seen to follow from the practical application of her philosophy, in writing produced by Rand herself, closer scrutiny is now surely required; the origins and implications of this, the quintessence of late capitalism's cultural logic, must at last be investigated thoroughly.

Having accepted Rand's place in the Lockean tradition there remain components in her writing which are curiously unlike anything else from across the spectrum of Anglo-American Liberal thought. The first to broach this controversial subject, political scholar and Libertarian theorist Chris Matthew Sciabarra has remarked that there are unlikely parallels between Rand's approach and that of Hegel and Marx: prompting him to speculate that, at some point in her development, Rand had absorbed key aspects of a specifically dialectic method of analysis. Sciabarra traces these elements in her fiction and philosophy to the period of her education in St. Petersburg – specifically, to the influence of her tutor N.O. Lossky, the most highly regarded Hegelian in Russia in that era.[12] Sciabarra has met with mixed responses. Not least because of Rand's implacable opposition to Hegel and Marx. But what if the 'Hegelian' components in her oeuvre identified by Sciabarra had been derived from sources that Rand had every reason to regard as antagonistic to Hegel? It is striking to note the extent to which *For the New Intellectual* (1960), for instance, parallels passages outlining the universal history of the individualist in *Der Einzige und seine Eigentum* (1844) – a book that attracted the enduring fury of Marx. Written by obscure nineteenth-century German philosopher Max Stirner, *The Ego and His Own* offers a uniquely egoist approach to the dialectical procedures favoured by Stirner's contemporaries. Despite being all but forgotten soon after its publication, Stirner's book enjoyed an unlikely revival of interest at the turn of the century right across Europe and America but especially in Russia. Might Stirner's book be a hitherto unacknowledged influence on the 'new concept of egoism' developed by Ayn Rand?[13]

On the face of it one might think such a conclusion far from surprising. 'Stirner is often taken to be the principal guiding text of individualist anarchism', remark Gerald F. Gaus and Fred D'Agostino in their introduction to Anarcho-Libertarian theory.[14] Indeed, one scholar goes so far as to describe the entire individualist tradition as just 'a footnote to Max Stirner'.[15] Stirnerian egoism is often thought

to have influenced early proponents of anarcho-individualism in
Europe (such as Emile Armand and Lev Chernyi) and America (such
as the editor of the journal *Liberty*, Benjamin Tucker), and is known
to have been read with interest by social anarchists, like Emma
Goldman.[16] His writings were cited by theorists working in post-war
movements which together make up the wave of countercultural
activity that is often taken to mark the post-modernist 'turn'. Despite
Albert Camus's negative appraisal in *The Rebel* (1951), Stirner
enjoyed a vogue among Existentialists, such as Henry Reed.[17] The
Situationist Raoul Vaneigem included Stirner in his select canon of
writers 'who have not yet played their last card in a game that we
have only just joined – the great gamble whose stake is freedom', in
The Revolution of Everyday Life (1967).[18] And the American anarcho-
communists 'For Ourselves: the Council For Generalized Self-
Management' make frequent reference to Stirner in their manifesto
entitled *The Right to be Greedy: Theses on the Practical Necessity of
Demanding Everything* (1974).[19] And post-structuralist theorists
have drawn on Stirner too: Gilles Deleuze, for instance, in *Logic of
Sense* (1969) quotes Stirner (in order to make much the same point
about Society and God as in the passage from Rand);[20] and Jacques
Derrida has Stirner in mind in his own belated contribution to this
body of political theory, *Specters of Marx* (1993).[21]

And yet the writer hailed by historians of political thought as
the fountainhead for these systems of post-modern philosophy
receives not the slightest attention in all the great many volumes
of critical material produced since the eighties that have tried and
failed to define what post-modernism (this impossible term coined
by Frederic Jameson) might mean exactly. And this is entirely

understandable; for the nature and the extent of Stirner's influence upon this wave of political philosophy is curiously difficult to quantify. As Gaus and D'Agostino point out, evidence of Stirner's impact on subsequent varieties of anarcho-individualism, for instance, is surprisingly slight, most thinkers either being unaware of Stirner or else rejecting him outright. 'Even the most prominent American Stirnerite, Benjamin Tucker, had already developed his anarchist systems in fairly full detail before reading Stirner'.[22] Rand conforms to this pattern. There is no evidence that Rand knew of Stirner before the sixties; at which point her viceroy Nathaniel Branden refers to the philosopher only in order to refute the suggestion that Rand's 'new concept of egoism' owes anything to those developed in the previous century by Nietzsche or Stirner.[23] As a result, Rand's philosophy finds no place in John F. Welsh's comprehensive and authoritative reception history, *Max Stirner's Dialectical Egoism: A New Interpretation* (2010). The suggestion that Stirner might have had a formative role (through Rand) in the development of 'the cultural logic of late capitalism' is therefore likely to be met with some degree of well-informed scepticism.

In fact, recent investigative work by historians of art may indicate that political historians have simply been looking in the wrong place and that the mainstream of the Stirnerian reception history is to be found, not in political philosophy, but in literature and art. The past few years have witnessed an explosion of interest in the long-overlooked impact of anarchism in art, with a series of exciting and revealing books on the topic appearing – including David Kadlec's *Mosaic Modernism: Anarchism, Pragmatism, Culture* (2000), Mark Antliff's and Patricia Leighton's *Cubism and Culture* (2001), Allan

Antliff's *Anarchy and Art* (2007), Theresa Papanikolas's *Anarchism and the Advent of Parisian Dada* (2010) and Nina Gurianova's *The Aesthetics of Anarchy: Art and Ideology in the Early Russian Avant-Garde* (2012). This new research establishes that the influence of anarchist political philosophy on Modernist Art (from right across America, Europe and Russia throughout the course of the twentieth century) is at once pervasive and profound. The possibilities opened up by this work are immense. But the pivotal part played by Stirnerian egoism across the newly discovered nexus of anarchist creativity must hold our attention here. Read in conjunction with other, often much earlier work by literary critics intrigued by obscure references to egoism in classics of literary Modernism, a clear pattern begins to emerge. In pioneering texts such as Robert Hallberg's *Canons* (1984), Bruce Clarke's *Dora Marsden and Early Modernism* (1996), Michael Levenson's *A Genealogy of Modernism* (1984), Paul Edwards's *Wyndham Lewis* (2000) and Jean-Michel Rabaté's *James Joyce and the Politics of Egoism* (2001), we encounter tantalizing glimpses of a forgotten reception history of dialectical egoism in literature and art. In this new context, it is possible to trace Rand's philosophy right back to a moment around the First World War when Stirner's *Der Einzige und sein Eigentum* held an extraordinary fascination for the European avant-garde; to perceive that, far from being post-modernist, much that we think of as synonymous with 'the cultural logic of late capitalism' has its inception in that brief phase of intense creative innovation we now call Modernism.

No doubt this suggestion must seem very unlikely to those who are familiar with received opinion on Modernism. Virtually a back-formation, created by practitioners and theorists associated with its self-declared successor, Modernism is often defined in relation to everything post-modernism is not. In books like Robert Venturi's post-modernist architectural manifesto *Learning from Las Vegas* (1977) and Frederic Jameson's *Post-Modernism* (1992), Modernism is presented as synonymous with those Grand Narratives that a contingent, practical and (purportedly) non-ideological post-modernism is described as being in reaction against. The philosophical underpinnings for Modernist experiment are thought to be either (1) the (radical) empirist tradition that inspired Marcel Proust's *La recherche de temps perdu* (1913–1927) and Gertrude Stein's *Making of Americans* (1925), or (2) the mainstream of (Hegelian) idealism, in which one might situate the intersubjectivity of T.S. Eliot's *The Waste Land* (1922) – or some tradition representing the admixture of these – that is to say, some total system of thought that requires disintegration of the individual subject into its social, psychological or biological components. 'The point I am struggling to attack', explains T.S. Eliot in his early essay 'Tradition and the Individual Talent' (1917), 'is perhaps related to the metaphysical theory of the substantial unity of the Soul'.[24] The fact that Eliot's rigorously impersonal manifesto appeared in the journal *The Egoist* is all too often permitted to pass unremarked. As Michael Levenson observed, in a prescient essay published over thirty years ago in *A Genealogy of Modernism*, the orthodox reading of Modernism is untenable: 'modernism was individualist before it was anti-individualist, anti-traditional before it was traditional, inclined to anarchism before it was inclined to authoritarianism'; and if critics have read the movement as anti-individualist, 'it is no doubt because the movement would go on to read itself that way'.[25]

But perhaps one can dismiss such evidence as mere anachronism, traces of a residual Romantic individualism? Levenson himself suggested that the early individualist Modernisms that interested him were displaced by the subsequent totalitarian varieties. In fact, this book will argue, closer scrutiny reveals that this unexpected Modernist individualism is something considerably more complex: a dialectical egoism that employs procedures derived from Hegel, which serves to set writing in this tradition apart from the near-contemporary vogue for Romantic egoism (reimagined by F.W. Nietzsche). The Radical Subjectivity pursued by writers and painters in the vanguard of Modernism is emphatically not that Transcendental Ego derived from Kantian philosophy which informs the poetry of Coleridge and Whitman; but a phenomenological or existential concept of self that can stand forth (ἔκστασις) from everything that it is, or rather everything that is its own, a perpetual self-analysis (ἀνάλυσις = unravelling) which preserves ego apart from its personal properties, its being in the world; that is to say, from every reification this nothing (the ego) might in the past have effected. Indeed, one can now begin to perceive why artists and writers of later generations, such as the Pop Artists at Britain's ICA, began, from the sixties on, to re-engage with the various lost possibilities presented by this preliminary Modernism. Far from signifying a regression to Romanticism on the part of these creators, their renewed interest in the literary and artistic achievements of 'individualist', or, rather more accurately, dialectical egoist, experiment reflects the extent to which Modernism pre-empts much that is often said to differentiate, from this earlier movement, post-modernist theory and practice.

The first chapter begins with the very latest and most exciting revisionist scholarship in this area, looking at the consensus beginning to emerge regarding the political significance of Dada. Long thought to be entirely apolitical, Dada is now known to have engaged heavily with the egoist philosophy of Stirner; and has accordingly been claimed for anarchism by contemporary historians of that movement. But, as Dora Marsden, the editor of the British Modernist publication *The Egoist*, pointed out at the start of the twentieth century (and to the chagrin of her anarchist contacts), Stirnerian egoism is ego-archist rather than an-archist; it cannot be defined by that movement, nor by any branch of that movement, precisely because anarchism is a movement (whatever the programme of political principles and no matter how loosely defined), and must therefore impinge upon the absolute freedom of the ego. This chapter introduces readers to *The Ego and His Own*, explaining why this book by Max Stirner, a companion of Marx and Engels, came to be forgotten so soon after its first publication, and revealing how his philosophy came to enjoy an extraordinary revival of interest at the start of the twentieth century. The chapter considers Stirner's reception history in France; the misinterpretation of his work by terror group the Bonnot Gang; and his subsequent impact upon Dada – and via Dada on contemporary conceptual art.

Chapter 2 sets out to chart the impact of Stirner's philosophy on Anglo-American literary Modernism – focussing on Dora Marsden – the inventor of suffragette street protest, editor of seminal Modernist magazine *The Egoist* and publisher of writers such as H.D., Ezra Pound, James Joyce and T.S. Eliot. This chapter reopens the long debate as to how much influence Marsden had on work appearing in her own journal, and shows how the Modernist material favoured by Marsden can be seen to fulfil her ambition for a literature that would realize an egoist psychology.

The third chapter follows through on the consequences of this new psychology, examining how Modernist writers Wyndham Lewis and James Joyce pursued alternative ways around the problems that sank Marsden: while Joyce embraced what Deleuze and Guattari later called the 'radical potential' of the Schizoid subject, Lewis developed a 'deadly' aesthetic that kept artistic ego distinct from properties that are its own, a creative project spanning decades that culminated in a brief unhappy flirtation with Nazism.

The final chapter is in a position to establish that Ayn Rand represents a final, belated, contribution to this Modernist experiment, a point that has significant consequences for understanding the cultural logic of late capitalism. This chapter blasts certain key assumptions concerning Rand's egoist philosophy held by a great many of those who have made her novel *The Fountainhead* the second-best seller in the United States (after the Bible). In this chapter, Rand's thought is shown to have drawn heavily on the Stirnerian egoist literature prevalent in Russia immediately prior to the Revolution. Written out of the histories by historians of the West and the East alike, the extraordinary achievements of individualist Russians in these years are at last coming to light – and this will have profound implications for admirers of Ayn Rand. Her innovations are considered in relation to previous literature in the Dialectical

Egoist tradition (outlined above), and though apparently slight, these innovations are shown to hold profound and troubling implications for those who commit themselves to Rand's new concept of egoism.

It has long been recognized that there are significant problems with the usual post-modernist perspective on Modernism. This book now shows precisely why. Presenting readers with a fresh perspective on the Modernist classics – as well as introducing less familiar art and writing that is only now beginning to attract interest in the West – this book offers a compelling re-evaluation of Modernism, of its 'selfish' streak. But if the implications for Modernist Studies are profound, there are also significant implications for how we understand the cultural logic of late capitalism. This new book challenges readers to undertake their own reappraisal of our very recent history, and to question the origin, interpretation and significance of 'rational self-interest', a philosophy that is coming to be regarded by many as a sort of common sense, an inevitable perspective on life, politics and business in the new global order.

1

THE NORTH POLE OF THE EGO

The Politics of Parisian Dada

'What Dada was in the beginning and how it developed is utterly unimportant in comparison with what it has come to mean in the mind of Europe.'[1] And what it has come to mean – in Berlin at least – is politics, according to Dadaist Richard Huelsenbeck – in his memoir of 1920, *En Avant Dada*. 'The true meaning of Dada was recognized only later in Germany by people who were zealously propagating it...', he claimed. 'While [Tristan] Tzara was still writing: "*Dada ne signifie rien*" – in Germany Dada lost its arts-for-arts-sake character with its very first movements ...' In Berlin, notes Huelsenbeck, Dada 'consciously adopted a political position', that position being 'radical Communism'.[2] This interpretation of Berlin Dada required the disparagement of its rival varieties, and Huelsenbeck likens the Galérie Dada in Zurich to 'a manicure salon of the fine arts, characterized by tea drinking old ladies trying to revive their vanishing sexual powers with the help of "something mad".'[3] The Dadaists of Paris and New York are – 'very nice and harmless looking gentlemen with pince-nez, horn-rimmed glasses and monocles, with flowing ties, faithful eyes and significant gestures, who can be seen from a distance to belong to literature'.[4]

Huelsenbeck's witty and spiteful disparagement of Parisian Dada, for his own polemical purpose, as apolitical, has been extremely influential, and lies behind many basic misconceptions regarding Dada's career in France and the United States that persist to this day. As Theresa Papanikolas observes, in her ground-breaking study *Anarchism and the Advent of Parisian Dada* (2010), 'Although historians of Paris Dada have always readily commented on the "anarchic" nature of such anti-art interventions, they have remained, with very few exceptions, silent about the real anarchist underpinnings of these direct assaults on institutional authority ... '.[5] In the classic statements on the subject by J.C. Middleton and Michel Sanouillet, Parisian Dada has been emphatically dismissed as an apolitical movement in the prehistory of Surrealism.[6] 'In any case, nothing transpired in the Dadaist documents of the epoch other than a coldly flaunted disdain for all political games and players', writes Sanouillet in *Dada à Paris* (1965). 'This indifference, surprising enough considering the vehement revolutionary and pacifist proclamations of the young Dadaists, distinguishes very neatly the Parisian movement from its Germanic counterparts ... It equally differentiates Dada from Surrealism, one of whose constants would be precisely this need for intervention in public affairs.'[7] And this view is reiterated in some of the more important recent research undertaken in this area: such as *The Dada Seminars* of 2005, and George Baker's *The Artwork Caught by His Tail: Francis Picabia and Dada in Paris* (2007). As Papanikolas explains, 'This paradoxical assumption that Paris Dada's "anarchy" was apolitical originates in the notion anarchism diminished during the First World War, when Marxism gained increasing hegemony on the left, and it has become axiomatic in formalist interpretations that analyze Dada "style" in opposition to Cubism, to place it in a continuum with Surrealism and ignore all three movements' historical contexts and political goals.'[8]

Pioneering research undertaken by Allan Antliff, in *Anarchy and Art* (2007), and by Papanikolas, in *Anarchism and the Advent of Parisian Dada* (2010), is at long last challenging this popular misconception. Both books seek to draw attention to the prevalence of anarchist theory on the left in the opening years of the twentieth century: and to the impact that this, now largely overlooked, political movement had upon leading writers and artists in the formative era of Modern Art. In this new historical context, Tristan Tzara's famous declaration that 'Dada ne signifie rien' suddenly acquires a rather different, and pointedly political, meaning... 'In contrast to socialism and communism – both of which preserved the state even as they granted the labor base varying degrees of governmental control – anarchism was the only left-wing philosophy to call for the elimination of all statist structures in favor of the complete sovereignty of the individual', notes Papanikolas. 'The Dadaists purposefully cultivated a chaotic atmosphere at the Cabaret Voltaire, inviting irony and rejecting all logic in order to attack the power structures responsible for the war and abolish their "rational" cultural codes.'[9] In fact, following the intervention of Papanikolas and Antliff it is difficult to understand how the specifically political aspect to the 'anarchy' fostered at Caberet Voltaire was ever overlooked. 'Let each man proclaim: there is a great, negative work of destruction to

be accomplished', declares Tzara, in his *Dada Manifesto*. 'Affirm the
cleanliness of the individual after the state of madness, aggressive
complete madness of a world abandoned to the heads of bandits,
who rend one another and destroy the centuries.'[10]

Antliff and Papanikolas establish that Dada retained this sense of
political purpose on moving to Paris and attracting young poets such
as André Breton and Louis Aragon: 'Through their poetry and prose,
art and notorious rebellious gestures, these writers and artists sought
to deconstruct the conformist mentality that celebrated war and
upheld bellicose nationalism.'[11] In their work, Parisian Dada emerges
as a manifestation of an anarcho-individualism prevalent, within the
much wider spectrum of anarchism, right across Europe in the period
prior to the First World War. But the pioneering work undertaken by
these two scholars must present us with new and profoundly difficult
questions concerning the reception history of Parisian Dada. Is the
pre-eminence of Marxism on the intellectual left in the inter-war era
really a sufficient reason for the enduring misinterpretation of that
movement? 'In reducing Paris Dada to a mere intellectual retreat, as
well as likening the movement's cultivation of individualism to the
capitalist possession of property, Huelsenbeck reflects the broader
contrasts between anarcho-individualism, anarcho-communism,
even Marxism, and he anticipates subsequent accounts of Paris Dada
informed by Marxist thought', writes Papanikolas.[12]

But if Huelsenbeck suggested that 'Parisian Dada was a by-
product of capitalism', he can hardly be held accountable for an
entire reception history that can only appear to vindicate such a
claim. 'Dada knew how to set the big rotary presses in motion ...'
observes Huelsenbeck. 'During the past decades in Europe, no

word, no concept, no philosophy, no slogan of party or sect can be said to have burst upon the imagination of a civilized society with such catastrophic force.'[13] Rather than rehearsing the usual tropes relating to capitalism's resilience in the face of attack, its capacity for co-opting the practices and iconography of movements opposed to it, or merely speculating that the 'wooden-horse' out the dictionary might yet prove to be a Trojan Horse all along, I want to suggest that, in this instance at least, the final result is not at all inconsistent with the philosophy underpinning Parisian Dada. I wish to argue that, though Antliff and Papanikolas are clear and emphatic when they note that a specific strain of anarcho-individualism, inspired by the German philosopher Max Stirner, 'diverged radically' from other anarchisms, they cannot but understate the true extent of that divergence. Each is engaged in recovering a history of anarchy in art, and though Stirner plays an important part in that history (having been taken as a key theorist of anarchism by artists and anarchists alike), there is good reason for wondering whether Stirnerian egoism might diverge sufficiently from other varieties of anarchism as to constitute something different entirely. Parisian Dada would have picked up on some components in Stirnerian theory, no doubt, and rejected the rest, presenting us with a loosely defined, synthetic, amalgam of 'anarchist' thought. But in work by writers and artists who made Stirner their special study the full implications of his egoist philosophy are thoroughly thought through, and I want to suggest that such work represents a serious obstacle to the emerging critical consensus. Beginning with a detailed overview of the Stirnerian philosophy and its historical context, this essay traces the impact of egoism on two of the pivotal figures in the Dada of Paris and New York – Marcel Duchamp and Francis Picabia. I hope to show that the accusations levelled at Parisian Dada by Huelsenbeck and subsequent Marxist critics represent an accurate, albeit instinctive, appreciation of the extent to which there is some parallel or relationship between Parisian Dada's ostensibly anarchist cultivation of individualism in art and the capitalist possession of property.

The ego and his own

On a hot August afternoon in 1896 the music critic James Huneker was standing in the Marktplatz at Bayreuth – when a member of the Wagner Theatre pointed to a house opposite, and said: 'Do you see that house with the double gables? A man was born there whose name will be green when Jean Paul and Richard Wagner are forgotten.' On learning that this name was Max Stirner – 'The crazy Hegelian' – Huneker registered incredulity and contempt: 'All fire and flame at that time for Nietzsche, I did not realize that the poet and rhapsodist had forerunners', he recalled. 'But Stirner displayed the courage of an explorer in search of the north pole of the Ego.'[14] Huneker would later present Stirner, in *Egoists: A Book of Supermen* (1909), as the culmination of an individualism that had emerged with the Romantic Movement, realized to varying degrees in the life and art of great intellects such as Stendhal, Baudelaire, Flaubert, Nietzsche, Blake and Ibsen. In his view, Stirner's one achievement, *Der Einzige und sein Eigentum* (1844), was the 'most revolutionary book ever written'. The claim cannot be easily dismissed. Stirner's philosophy went beyond anything produced by his contemporaries working within and against Hegelian theory: a rigorous, systematic act of deconstruction that has been said to have anticipated later important trends in Western philosophy, including individualist anarchism, psychoanalysis, existentialism and post-modernism.[15]

Little is known about the man who called himself Max Stirner. The information that we do have was uncovered, with considerable difficulty, between thirty and forty years after his death, by John Henry Mackay (the German anarchist with a Scottish name) and published in *Max Stirner: Sein Leben und sein Werk* in 1898. He reveals that 'Max Stirner' was a fictional entity, a nom de guerre. The figure behind this persona was born Johann Caspar Schmidt on 6 November 1806 in the Bavarian town of Bayreuth. He was the son of a flute-maker, who died six months after Schmidt's birth. In 1809 his mother remarried and moved to Kulm in West Prussia, leaving Schmidt with his godfather, an apothecary. He proved an industrious student, going on to study philosophy at the University of Berlin where he would meet Ludwig Feuerbach and attend lectures given by G.W.F. Hegel. But Schmidt left Berlin before taking final examinations to look after his mother during her final illness. He returned to Berlin in 1832, but failed to complete his studies or to secure the paid teaching position he sought. The death of his mother was followed by that of his godfather and his new bride, who died in childbirth in August 1838. A year later Schmidt finally secured paid teaching work at a private school for young ladies from upper-class families run by a Madame Gropius. Up to this time Schmidt's life had been one continuous record of poverty, loss and lonely study.

But here, unknown to his employer, Schmidt fashioned for himself in secrecy a new identity. Taking up his nickname at university – a playful reference to the unusually high span of his forehead – he transformed himself into 'Max Stirner', a serious writer and participant in the circle of radical thinkers who would meet in a Weinstube called Hippel's on Friedrichstrasse every evening in the early 1840s to discuss the formulation of a philosophy that might provide the basis for the political and cultural revolution of Prussia and Europe. Karl Marx and Friedrich Engels, Ludwig Feuerbach, notorious atheist theologians Bruno and Edgar Bauer, Moses Hess – all spent nights here engaging in intense arguments over the future of post-Hegelian thought. Stirner's friend Edgar Bauer would recall that Stirner was an 'amiable and unobtrusive person, never offensive nor striving after brilliant effects in either phrase, conduct, or appearance'.[16] None of his friends there seem to have anticipated the *untergang* that followed. But in 1843 everything changed. Stirner remarried an 'advanced' young woman called Marie Dähnhardt. He was rumoured to be working on a 'great philosophic work'. Then, in October 1844, Schmidt resigned from his post at the girls' school, *Der Einzige und sein Eigentum* was published in Leipzig and people throughout the German States were suddenly aware of a monstrous philosopher of selfishness called *Max Stirner*.

The sensation was short-lived. The book was banned, and eclipsed by political revolution in 1848. Max Stirner's fame was over in a moment – and the one great love of his life had gone too. The woman to whom he had dedicated his book, 'My Sweetheart, Marie Dähnhardt', had left, moving to London, where she supported herself by writing. On being tracked to Australia by Mackay in 1897 and asked for information on Stirner, she would only reply that her husband had been too much of an egotist to keep friends, and was 'very sly'. His old friends at Hippel's seldom saw him after this. Stirner had retreated into poverty and solitude. He died at the age of fifty of fever contracted from an insect's bite. 'To Mackay's labours', remarks James Huneker, 'we owe all we know of a man who was as absolutely swallowed up by the years as if he had never existed'.[17]

The self-created entity that one encounters in *Der Einzige und sein Eigentum* is something very different. 'Nothing is more to me than myself!' Stirner begins. The Good Cause, whether God or Man or State, cares nothing for the individual upon whom each calls to make sacrifice; each is the embodiment of self-interest, itself a perfect egoist. Stirner will take a lesson from them, 'and propose, instead of further unselfishly serving those great egoists, rather to be the egoist myself'.[18]

The book that follows is divided into two parts, 'Man' and 'I'. In the first Stirner offers phenomenological accounts of egoism, reiterating the grand narratives produced by his mentor Hegel in *Phenomenology of Mind* (1807) and *Lectures on the Philosophy of World History* (1837) – only to undermine Hegel's conclusion that the formation of consciousness and the movement of world history both have their end in the Absolute Idea.

The psychological development of the subject is instead conceived of as a combat of *self-assertion*. 'From the moment he catches sight of the light of the world a man seeks to find out *himself* and get hold of *himself* out of its confusion, in which he, with everything else, is tossed about in motley mixture... But everything that comes in contact with the child defends itself in turn against his attacks, and asserts its own persistence.'[19]

The victory of every child is the triumph of Mind; 'the world is discredited, for we are above it, we are mind.'[20] But in conquering the physical, in finding himself as Mind, the youth is losing himself to the power of Mind, submitting himself a sacrifice to pre-existing systems of thought. 'As in childhood one had to overcome the resistance of the *laws of the world*, so now in everything that he proposes he is met by an objection of the mind, of reason, of his *own conscience.*'[21] In Stirner's view, the youth becomes a man when capable of taking the world as it is, instead of fancying it amiss and wanting to improve it, to model it after an ideal – beyond thesis and antithesis to the synthesis, treating the ideal as equally nothing with the physical, and dealing with both according to his own interest. 'As I find myself back of things, and that as mind, so I must later find myself also back of thoughts – to wit, as their creator and *owner.*'[22] Stirner's mock-Hegelian dialectic renders the Idea no longer absolute but subject to the individual will. 'In the time of spirits thoughts grew till they overtopped my head, whose offspring they yet were; they hovered about me and convulsed me like fever-phantasies – an awful power... And now I take the world as what it is to me, as *mine*, as my property; I refer all to myself.'[23]

The world history that follows Stirner's psychological account of the dialectical movement towards egoism is comparatively messy and unconvincing – and was singled out for especially harsh criticism by Marx and Engels for precisely this reason – but that is perhaps part of the point. An accurate, integrated grand-narrative would be incompatible with Stirner's aggressive demolition of every totalitarian idea. He himself seems to acknowledge the irony of the enterprise in the admission that 'The historical reflections... which I propose to insert episodically at this place are not given with the claim of thoroughness, or even of approved soundness, but solely because it seems to me that they may contribute toward making the rest clear.'[24] Hegel offered a philosophy of world history that moved through three phases: 'The East knew, and to the present day knows, only that *One* is free; the Greek and Roman world, that *some* are free; the German world knows that *All* are free.' In Stirner the history of the world began with a 'Negroid age', the time of dependence on things, the second age is that of the 'Mongoloid', the time of dependence on thoughts, while the coming, third age is that of the Caucasian, of self-interest.

Fortunately, perhaps for the reasons suggested, Stirner puts little emphasis on this ridiculous and offensive historical framework, repeatedly veering off into visceral attacks upon humanist and socialist thought, with Ludwig Feuerbach's *Essence of Christianity* (1841) being subjected to particularly rigorous criticism. 'What he says is that we had only mistaken our own essence, and therefore looked for it in the other world, but that now, when we see that God was only our human essence, we must recognize it again as ours and move it back out of the other world into this.'[25] In Stirner's view, humanist thought is only the latest reiteration of the Christian religion. 'The supreme being is indeed the essence of man, but, just because it is his *essence* and not he himself, it remains quite immaterial whether we see it outside him and view it as "God", or find it in him and call it "Essence of Man" or "Man". I am neither God nor *Man*, neither the supreme essence nor my essence, and therefore it is all one in the main whether I think of the essence as in me or outside me.'[26] In Stirner's view, this emphasis upon the essential qualities of the Human must inevitably lead to the oppression of those people who fail to measure up to the criteria set out by well-meaning humanists like Bruno Bauer – who had controversially argued that Jews should be denied political rights if they failed to embrace their full humanity by refusing to relinquish an exclusive and outmoded religion. 'Because you have discovered the idea of humanity, does it follow from this that each Jew can become a convert to it?' demands Stirner. 'Rather therefore, invert the case, and say to yourself, *I am a human being*! I do not need to begin by producing the human being in myself, for he belongs to me already, like all my qualities.'[27]

'Every higher essence', writes Stirner, 'such as truth, mankind, and so on, is an essence *over* us.'[28] The French revolutionaries served Man – and cut off the heads of men. Liberals had overthrown monarchies so that all might rule – but no one person is All. The Socialists wanted to abolish personal property to create a society in which everyone is equal – but there is no such thing as society. Result: 'Neither command nor property is left to the individual; the State took the former, society the latter.'[29] The first half of Stirner's book presents a compelling vision of a world grown insubstantial, haunted by the spectres of essentialist thought, by spooks that had sucked themselves full, on the blood of each living subject, to the point of being made corporeal. 'Man, your head is haunted; you have wheels in your head!'[30]

In the second part of his book, Stirner makes an impassioned plea for individual power over any rights – and for personal property over any freedom – conferred by the State. 'It is not recognized in the full amplitude of the word that all freedom is essentially – self-liberation – that I can have only so much freedom as I procure for myself.'[31] The State may set a man free but if the man is possessed by that State's ideology he is only set free to obey. Freedom is self-liberation or nothing at all. 'My freedom becomes complete only when it is my – *might*; but by this I cease to be a merely free man, and become an own man.'[32] A mere idea, freedom can mean nothing without the power that comes with ownership. 'I am free from what I am *rid* of, owner of what I have in my *power* or what I *control*.'[33] Stirner's book is therefore a manifesto for insurrection rather than a revolution. 'The former consists in an overturning of conditions, of the established condition or status, the State or society, and is accordingly a political or social act; the latter has indeed for its unavoidable consequence a transformation of circumstances, yet does not start from it but from men's discontent with themselves, is not an armed rising, but a rising of individuals.'[34] In contrast to most forms of anarchist theory, Stirner's does not advocate the abolition of the State as an end in itself. It is already dead to the egoist. And must wither away as an increasing number of egoists inside the system manipulate the rest in their own self-interest, refusing to acknowledge and support the collective good. 'I, the egoist, have not at heart the welfare of this "human society"', explains Stirner, 'I sacrifice nothing to it, I only utilize it; but to be able to utilize it completely I transform it rather into my property and my creature; that is, I annihilate it, and form in its place the *Union of Egoists*.'[35]

It is hard to say what this phrase might mean – as Stirner's new world flickers in and out of focus across a long and disjointed series of deconstructive readings. But this vagueness is surely necessary to Stirner's project. 'The Revolution aimed at new arrangements', he writes; 'insurrection leads us no longer to let ourselves be arranged, but to arrange ourselves, and sets no hopes on "institutions" '.[36] Should the coming age see egoists coming into their own the consequences must necessarily be at once radical – and utterly inconsistent. As if to prove this point, Stirner devotes a considerable passage to praising the example of Jesus Christ, after spending much of the book vituperating Christianity in all its permutations. 'Perhaps I too, in the very next moment, defend myself against my former thoughts; I too am likely to change suddenly my mode of action; but not on account of its not corresponding to Christianity, not on account of its affronting the idea of mankind, humanity, and humanitarianism, but – because I am no longer all in it, because it no longer furnishes me any full enjoyment, because I doubt the earlier thought or no longer please myself in the mode of action just now practiced.'[37]

Because Stirner's ego is not an Absolute Idea. 'When Fichte says, "The ego is all", this seems to harmonize perfectly with my thesis', notes Stirner. 'But it is not that the ego is all, but the ego *destroys* all.'[38] His ego is no repetition in the finite mind of the infinite I AM, the transcendent ego of the Romantic Movement; 'for "being" is abstraction, as is even "the I" '.[39] In Stirner's manifesto, 'ego' is singularity, not species – 'I am not an ego along with other egos, but the sole ego: I am unique.'[40] Furthermore Stirner is clear this individual selfhood is neither self-consistent nor constant; 'only the self-dissolving ego, the never-being ego, the *finite* ego is really I.'[41] This ego is provisional, contingent. Produced anew from one moment to the next. 'I do not presuppose myself', he insists, 'because I am every moment just positing or creating myself, and I am only by being not presupposed but posited, and, again, posited only in the moment when I posit myself; that is, I am creator and creature in one.'[42] For his ego is not an idea but that *nothing* he must be in the moment he considers everything that he is. 'If I set my cause on myself, the unique one', Stirner concludes, 'then my cause is set upon my transitory, mortal creator, my self consuming, and I might say: I have set my cause upon nothing.'[43]

None of Stirner's contemporaries seem to have understood (or – been prepared to accept) the extent to which this egoism marked a break with essentialist thought. In their written responses, Ludwig Feuerbach, Moses Hess and Bruno Bauer, all portray Stirner's ego as another manifestation of the Absolute Idea. In the most extensive, most influential, response to Stirner's book, Karl Marx and Friedrich Engels even depict the author as 'Saint Max', a theologian at a Council of the Early Church, pronouncing an anathema on the heretics among the Young Hegelians; the point being that for all Stirner had to say against the spirit-world of the Berlin School, he had not taken what Marx and Engels viewed as the logical next step – to a materialist philosophy, requiring active rather than theoretical struggle. In reproducing the structure of Stirner's book, in obsessively detailed, line-by-line refutation, Marx and Engels sneer that 'The "book" itself is divided like the book "of old", into the Old and New Testament – namely, into the unique history of man (the Law and the Prophets) and the inhuman history of the unique (the Gospel of the Kingdom of God)'.[44] Having undertaken substantial research into the role played by changing modes of production upon social relations, Marx and Engels are,

understandably, impatient with Stirner's fast and loose approach
to empirical proofs. They note that Stirner had failed to regard the
extent to which his notion of individual selfhood was determined
by material conditions, product of a specific historical era. 'Since
Saint Max pays no attention to the physical and social "life" of the
individual, and says nothing at all about "life", he quite consistently
abstracts from historical epochs, nationalities, classes, etc.'[45] The
concept of property underpinning the theory of self-liberation
is similarly regarded as the result of etymological abstraction:
'"Stirner" refuted the communist abolition of private property
by first transforming private property into "having", and then
declaring the verb "to have" an indispensable word, an eternal truth,
because even in communist society it could happen that Stirner will
"have" a stomach-ache'.[46] In fact, Stirner had merely followed Hegel
in making a speculative idea, an abstract conception, the driving
force of history. 'Thus, history becomes a mere history of illusory
ideas, a history of spirits and ghosts, while the real, empirical
history that forms the basis of this ghostly history is only utilized
to provide bodies for these ghosts; from it are borrowed names
required to clothe these ghosts with the appearance of reality. In
making this experiment our saint frequently forgets his role and
writes an undisguised ghost-story'.[47] Ultimately Marx and Engels
reject Stirner's claim that there is nothing to say about the unique
because it is a corporeal, not constructed individual, asserting that
'the matter here is rather the same as in the case of Hegel's absolute
idea at the end of the *Logik* and of absolute personality at the end
of the *Encyklopaedie*, about which there is likewise nothing to say
because the construction contains everything that can be said about

such constructed personalities'.[48] In their view, Stirner had only succeeded in transforming into an extremely clumsy and confused idea what Hegel had previously said concerning the Doctrine of Essence; in the course of repeating this, failing to recognize that 'he, as mere "posited" ego, as creation, i.e., insofar as he possesses *existence*, is merely a *seeming* ego, and he is "*essence*", *creator*, only insofar as he does *not* exist, but only imagines himself'.[49] But this is precisely what Stirner would appear to be trying to convey. The most radical element in Stirner's egoist philosophy is dismissed by Marx and Engels in *Die Deutsche Ideologie* as nothing but 'juggling tricks on the tightrope of the objective'. [50] Stirner is presented as a latter-day Don Quixote, in spiritual combat with phantasmal foes, only choosing to do so, not from knightly altruism, but from the greedy self-interest of that incipient bourgeois – Sancho Panza!

In the opinion of John F. Welsh, 'The deference that Marxists, critical theorists, postmodernists, and poststructuralists confer on Marx's account of Stirner in *The German Ideology* is a fascinating study in the clout wielded by ideologies that have been institutionalized in political movements, popular culture, and the halls of academe.'[51] Herbert Read offers a case in point. In an otherwise intelligent and informed appraisal of Stirner's achievement in *The Tenth Muse* (1957), Read remarks that '*Der Einzige und sein Eigentum* as Stirner's book was called, hardly survived Marx's onslaught.'[52] In fact, the efficacy of *The German Ideology* was entirely nullified by the decision not to pursue publication following an initial rejection. Marx would later remember that 'We abandoned the manuscript to the gnawing criticism of the mice all the more willingly as we had achieved our main purpose – self-clarification.'[53] Nearly one

hundred years would pass before *The German Ideology* would at last
be published by the Institute of Marxism-Leninism in the Soviet
Union in 1932. The delay would have far-reaching and long-lasting
repercussions. It is hard to imagine Stirner would have enjoyed his
later vogue with the revolutionary left had it been known that Marx
and Engels had damned him as a 'petty bourgeois individualist
intellectual'. Whatever Stirner's radical pretensions, Marx and
Engels show the practical effect of his theory must prove 'wholly
conservative'.[54] In a letter to Marx, 19 November 1844, Engels
had complained that 'This egoism is simply the essence of present
society and present man brought to consciousness, the ultimate
that can be said against us by present society, the culmination of all
the theory intrinsic to the prevailing stupidity.'[55] With the failure to
publish *The German Ideology*, the uncompromising views held by
Marx and Engels were forgotten. And when *Der Einzige und sein
Eigentum* began again to be read by advanced groups of artists and
political activists, in Western Europe, North America and Russia, in
the years running up to the turn of the century, the book could be
regarded as a natural supplement or alternative to the revolutionary
programme of Marx.

The rise of egoism in pre-war France

Egoism first returned to prominence in Western Europe (following
translations of Stirner's masterwork by R.L. Reclaire and Henri
Lasvignes as *L'Unique et sa propriété* in 1899 and 1900) – on the
back of a criminal rampage. Led by Jules Bonnot, a car mechanic

and professional criminal from Lyon, the Bonnot Gang took their inspiration from Albert Libertad, the editor of the journal *l'anarchie*, the only anarchist paper in the Republic at that time which positively promoted crime as a form of political rebellion through a controversial 'illegalist' reading of Stirner.[56] Intent on developing an entirely new mode of criminal activity that fully exploited the latest innovations in industrial technology in order to realise crime's *spectacular* potential, the Bonnot Gang pulled off a series of high-profile bank heists, car thefts, and drive-by shootings in France and Belgium, utilizing high-tech weaponry (automatic firearms) and powerful automobiles (two stolen Delaunay-Bellevilles and a De Dion Bouton).[57] Their robberies immediately fired the public imagination – reenacted for film within hours of their occurring and shown in musically accompanied newsreels throughout Paris. The ringleaders, Bonnot and Garnier, were themselves, certainly, quick to explore their new cult of celebrity and the extraordinary opportunities presented by the mass media, posting propaganda to the press and even on one occasion dictating a message at gunpoint to journalists in the offices of the *Petit Parisien*.[58] 'I know there will be an end to this struggle that has begun between me and the formidable arsenal at Society's disposal', Garnier remarked in his press release. 'I know that I will be beaten, I am the weakest; but I sincerely hope to make you pay dearly for your victory.'[59] In fact, Bonnot would meet his end a month later in the 'Red Nest' at Choisy in a storm of gunfire and dynamite, and Garnier at the siege at Nogent, killed by a newly militarized police force, packing machine guns, motorized transport and melanite explosives. But the last stand was captured on film – and thousands came to see the struggle between the individual and society replayed in a popular

Parisian cinema, in what must surely count as some of the earliest *cinema vérité*.[60] 'I allow nobody the right to impose their will on me, no matter what the pretext', wrote Garnier, in a manuscript found on his body by the police.

> I don't see why I shouldn't have the right to eat some grapes or apples just because they're the property of Mr X.... What has he done that I haven't that makes him the sole beneficiary? I say – nothing – and therefore I have the right to satisfy my need, and if he wants to stop me by force, I will revolt, and oppose my strength to his, as, being attacked, I will defend myself by whatever means possible.[61]

As Richard Parry observes, in his gripping account of *Les bandits en auto*, 'Until the advent of the Bonnot Gang, the Anarchist-individualists had been largely ignored or ridiculed as inconsequential by the wider Anarchist movement, but now [the latter] were forced to devote time and space to demonstrating that illegalism and anarchism had nothing in common.'[62] 'Illegalism explains itself, perhaps even justifies itself in theory', wrote Mauricius, new editor of the journal *l'anarchie*; 'in practice is it not too weak to live openly, outside of codes? Can economic emancipation only be made en masse? And will the revolutionary cohorts not take advantage of individual outlaws? Agonizing questions whose solution is in the blood of so many men of courage and of valor.'[63] And in fact Mauricius is probably correct to insist that to miss or to discount the impractical aspects to a life living out *grand theft auto* must constitute a serious misreading of Stirner. Like the State, Law presents the egoist with too many protections and opportunities to justify such blanket refusal. In the coming, Third

Age envisaged by Stirner the Law would probably exist, but would be recognized for what it is; that is to say, an unjust system of competing interests that offers prizes and pitfalls: to be praised in public, ignored in secret, exploited where possible and resisted whenever it gets in the way.

In spite of this fact, the Bonnot Gang were blamed squarely on the individualist current by the wider anarchist movement, which had, rather belatedly, realized that Stirner's recognition of *property* is incompatible with Proudhon's belief that *property is theft*. 'Such actions have nothing anarchist about them, they are actions which are purely and simply bourgeois', wrote Jean Grave (one of the thirty defendants in the *Trial of Thirty*; sometimes called 'Pope' of the anarchist movement).[64] 'Their actions proceeded from a capitalist mentality which has as its end the amassing of money and leading a parasitic life', argued Alfred Rosmer; 'they are pseudo-anarchists who dishonour the fine anarchistic ideal', concluded Gustave Hervé.[65] The anarchist reaction culminated in the expulsion/ walkout of the anarcho-individualist party from the congress held by the *Fédération Communiste Révolutionnaire Anarchistes* in August 1913. 'Jean Grave threatened to leave if they did not, so the individualists walked out, declaring the congress authoritarian and anti-Anarchist. For their part, the conference condemned all forms of individualism as bourgeois and incompatible with anarcho-communism.'[66]

In spite – or rather because – of this disavowal, the Stirnerian faction would eventually emerge as the pre-eminent movement within anarchism in the years following the First World War – as support for what had been the mainstream of anarchism shifted to parties that had taken an uncompromising line on participating in an imperial power struggle. As Parry explains:

> Kropotkin, Grave, Hervé, Paul Reclus and Charles Malato, who had not hesitated to condemn the Bonnot Gang for killing proletarians and robbing banks, aligned themselves behind the Allies – Russia, France and Great Britain – who, in turn, did not hesitate to squander sixty thousand lives in a single day if it aided their fight for imperialist plunder. Despite the years of resistance to militarism, most syndicalist and anarchist militants of military age went to the colours without resistance; the State did not even need to round-up all those 'subversives' on the Carnet B – a list of those thought to pose a threat to the effective mobilization of working class support for the war.[67]

As a direct result, disenchanted anarchists began to align themselves with the Bolsheviks, who had won the revolution in the East, or the discredited Stirnerian egoists, who had rejected the notion of self-sacrifice for any cause out of hand. Largely overlooked by historians, this brief and problematic subversion of mainstream anarchism in interwar Europe was to have lasting repercussions for politics in the West, through its formative impact on the new forms of art and literature termed Modernist. As researchers of the era are increasingly beginning to realize, the politics of pioneering movements such as Futurism, Vorticism and Dadaism were heavily influenced by the vogue for anarcho-individualism, with the radical philosophy of Max Stirner seeming to possess some particular appeal.

Papanikolas has established why this might be the case in her ground-breaking study of the anarchist component in Dada.

In contrast to the new proletarian art prescribed by the Third International, Stirnerian egoism required that the artist create exclusively according to their own agenda, and put a premium on formal innovation. 'Many anarcho-individualists pointed out that such uncompromised self-expression, far from suggesting a purely aesthetic retreat into a realm of "life-less" symbols, was a quintessentially anti-authoritarian gesture and thus a cerebral manifestation of revolt', observes Papanikolas.[68] And the most powerful post-war articulation of the revolutionary significance of such complete creative freedom is said to have come from critic Florent Fels, who located intellectual revolution in the personal liberation implicit in formal experiment.[69] In modern literature and art appearing right across Europe, Fels perceived a new spirit that perfectly encapsulated a specifically Stirnerian philosophical approach to being in the world. 'Modern poetry', writes Fels in anarchist journal *La Mêlée* in 1918, 'in reaction against all attempts at the scientific explanation of the world, affirms itself as antididactic, the enemy of declamation, of description, of symbols, of the great imperatives, of what is traditionally the poetic expression of the mind'.[70] Having located revolution in creative innovation, this Stirnerian egoist reasoned that the new wave of artists, together with their counterparts in science, would transform society through uncompromising, creative expression of their own uniqueness. To further this end, Fels launched artistic and literary review *Action* in February 1920, publishing poetry, fiction, criticism and art, by Cubist and Dadaist critics and poets, together with work by Stirnerian writers, such as Dora Marsden, British editor of *The Egoist*.[71] There was thus a substantial Stirnerian party active within the wider anarchist community in Paris by the time Tristan Tzara came to that city, predisposed to welcome the Dadaists in the belief that their new approach to art encapsulated a specifically Stirnerian mode of political revolt.

The politics of Dada

With the version of Dada that Tzara brought to Paris, Fels got rather more than he had bargained for. '[Dada] expresses the knowledge of a supreme egoism, in which laws wither away', declared the *Dada Manifesto* of 1918. 'On the one hand: tottering world in flight, betrothed to the glockenspiel of hell. On the other hand: new men; rough, bouncing, riding on hiccups.'[72] In fact, as Huber van der Berg first revealed, in *Avantgarde und Anarchismus: Dada in Zurich and Berlin* (1987), Zurich Dada had strong roots in the anarchist milieu, with key founder Hugo Ball possessing an expert knowledge of Bakunin. And though van der Berg believed that Ball had relinquished any serious interest in politics long before the opening of Cabaret Voltaire, Papanikolas has shown that Ball's rejection of Bakunin did not indicate he had rejected anarchism altogether: for his knowledge of anarchist theory included the various philosophies underpinning anarcho-individualism. 'Not only had Ball written his doctoral dissertation on Nietzsche', she observes, 'he had also moved in [...] circles associated with the magazines *Die Aktion* and *Der Storm*, where writers and artists inspired by Nietzsche and Stirner were formulating an anarcho-individualist alternative to revolutionary anarchism.'[73] The poems Ball performed nightly at the Cabaret Voltaire must be understood, not, as van der Berg would have it, as some apolitical attempt to save language, but as a politically motivated assault upon the corrupt language underpinning modern society (thereby effecting real social renewal in the manner prescribed by Stirner – through an insurrection effected upon the level of the individual consciousness):

gadji beri bimba

giandridi lauli lonni cadori

gadjama bim beri glassala

glandridi glassala tuffum i zimbrabim

blassa glassasa tuffum i zimbrabim.[74]

This is what Tzara brought to Paris following the expulsion of the egoist faction by the anarcho-communist contingent, a short-lived splinter group Radical Dada or Bund Revolutionärer Künstler, in the course of a dispute that echoed the great schism that opened up, throughout Europe, within anarchist communities during the war. In Zurich, Tzara had built on Ball's theory of an insurrection of the word, refining the Stirnerian impetus behind, what he saw, as that great, negative work of destruction. 'The new artist protests: he no longer paints (symbolic and illusionist reproduction) but creates – directly in stone, wood, iron, tin, boulders – locomotive organisms capable of being turned in all directions by the limpid wind of momentary sensation', said Tzara, in *Dada Manifesto* 1918. 'All pictorial or plastic work is useless: let it then be a monstrosity that frightens servile minds.'[75] As Georges Ribemont-Dessaignes explained, 'There is a religion of Art, like there is a religion of God.' And if the concept of Art is another *essence* raised over us, the Stirnerian egoist must destroy every manifestation of art, including his own, perpetually

asserting the absolute authority of ego, through a continual negation
of the art-object, and its re-cognition as property. 'Destroy what you
construct if you need to construct', insists Ribemont-Dessaignes.
'Dada will destroy Dada. You construct nothing that is not rotten'.[76]
Thus, Louis Aragon at the Second Dada Matinee (5 February 1920)
recited his 'Manifesto of the Dada Movement':

> No more painters, no more men of letters, no more musicians,
> no more sculptors, no more religions, no more republicans, no
> more royalists, no more imperialists, no more anarchists, no
> more socialists, no more Bolsheviks, no more politicians, no more
> proletariat, no more democrats, no more bourgeois, no more
> aristocrats, no more armies, no more police, no more countries,
> enough then of these imbecilities no more nothing no more
> nothing, *nothing, nothing, nothing, nothing.*[77]

In practice (as Huelsenbeck pointed out) despite such rhetoric, the
pictorial and plastic material produced by Dadaists in Zurich and
Paris did not, for the most part, differ significantly from the new
modes of painting and sculpture developed by Italian Futurists,
French Cubists and German Expressionists. 'Tzara and Ball founded
a "gallery" in which they exhibited Dadaistic art, i.e., "modern"
art, which for Tzara meant non-objective abstract art', remembers
Huelsenbeck. 'Things came to such a pass that they borrowed
pictures from the Berlin art-dealer Herwarth Walden (who for a long
time had been making money out of abstract art theories) and passed
them off on the Swiss pudding-heads as something extraordinary.'[78]
Even Tzara's *new medium*, 'enthusiastically touted', in *Dada Manifesto
1918*, as the *non plus ultra* of the 'most modern' painting, can be seen

to have built upon the technical experiments of Pablo Picasso: 'He began to stick sand, hair, post-office forms and pieces of newspaper onto his pictures', remembers Huelsenbeck, 'to give them the value of a direct reality, removed from everything traditional'.[79]

Yet *found objects* or *ready-mades* must encapsulate something of that egoism specific to Dadaism. In the writing of Antliff and Papanikolas the *object portraits* of French artist Francis Picabia, for instance, are said to mark a definitive shift from Formalism to egoist Dada in New York and Paris. In each case, industrial, mass-produced items are abstracted from their everyday context, and presented under allusive titles as objects of art; the *Portrait d'une jeune fille Americaine dans l'état de nudité* (1915) being a diagrammatic plan of a spark-plug inscribed FOR-EVER, and the *Nature Mortes: Portrait de Cézanne, Portrait de Rembrandt, Portrait de Renoir* (1920) – a lewd toy monkey attached to a piece of cardboard. 'These depictions are rightly singled out because they embody so many of the definitive features of Dadaist production in New York', writes Antliff, in relation to the five object portraits published in the July-August issue of the art journal *291* in 1915: 'in that their evocation of industrialism and commercialism violate conventions defining art while simultaneously setting off a chain of associative readings that transgressed the subject at hand'.[80] And Antliff has established that this turn from Formalism to the 'new medium' in Picabia's oeuvre was motivated by the artist's discovery of Stirnerian egoism in 1912: 'The impetus can be traced to a second ex-cubist, Marcel Duchamp', explains Antliff. 'He and Picabia were very close, and upon returning to Paris that fall [1912], they likely discussed Stirner's ideas at length. In any event, scarcely three months later, Picabia was introducing New Yorkers to "the mysterious feelings of his ego" in free-flowing expressions "cut loose" from cubist "convention" and its "established body of laws and accepted values".[81] And, as Papanikolas notes, in a discussion of object portraits displayed at the Dada Manifestation at Maison de l'Oeuvre in 1920, echoes of this engagement with Stirner persist in the articles and manifestos Picabia published in Paris during the twenties, in which he defines Dadaism in Stirnerian terminology as the negation of belief systems, chauvinistic ideas and ideologies: [82]

> Dada feels nothing for it is nothing, nothing, nothing.
>
> It is like your hopes: nothing
>
> like your paradise: nothing
>
> like your idols: nothing
>
> like your political men: nothing
>
> like your heroes: nothing
>
> like your artists: nothing
>
> like your religions: nothing.[83]

But how can Picabia's object portraits be said to embody Stirnerian insurrection in particular, given that iconoclasm is, to varying degrees, endemic right across the new modes of art that appear in this period? Neither Antliff nor Papanikolas are clear on this important point – and I suggest that this is down to a misreading of Stirner, a misreading that permits both cultural historians to regard this egoist philosophy as in some way congruent with the versions of anarchism developed by Proudhon, Bakunin, Kropotkin, etc., etc. 'Max Stirner's anarchist-individualist manifesto, *The Ego and Its Own*, [is] a *materialist* critique of metaphysics […]', explains Antliff, and this belief that Stirner's break with Hegelian Idealism *must be a materialism* informs a critical reading of Picabia's five object portraits that presents these pieces as a reconnect with the physical. 'Combatting metaphysics, Stirner countered that ideas are indelibly grounded in our corporeal being', writes Antliff.[84] And this would seem to be how Papanikolas too, has interpreted Stirner, given her contention this philosophy is consistent with an art movement that, in her view, sought to circumvent systems and theories through a surrender to something as entirely objective as the 'anti-law' of chance.– 'The importance of chance to Dada was documented in such collages as Arp's *Untitled (Squares Arranged According to the Laws of Chance)*', she writes, 'in which [Arp] evaded the constraints of conscious art-making by dropping bits of paper onto a surface and adhering them wherever they fell'.[85] If this be correct, Dadaism's object portraits are rather more like those *Nature-Mortes* produced by that Formalist Picasso than one might expect: as Huelsenbeck says, these too represent a search for 'a new, direct reality'.[86] But, as Marx and Engels categorically established, Stirner's egoism *is not a materialism*. Indeed, in Stirner's view such a move would represent an undesirable reversion to an earlier stage of being – that physical tyranny from which the ego eventually escapes – into the Spirit. The pronounced subjectivity evident in Dada experiment is no sufficient reason for considering it Stirnerian. If the *ready-mades* synonymous with Dadaism really do represent a re-engagement with material reality, such *subjectivity* merely makes it a *Radical Empiricism*. Indeed, it is tempting to interpret those Dadaist 'cut-ups' proposed by Tzara in precisely this way, given the centrality of this method for subsequent movements such as Surrealism and Beat. As is well known, the 'cut ups' created by David Gascoyne and William Burroughs have their ultimate source in Tzara, his *Dada Manifesto* on 'Feeble Love and Bitter Love: VIII – To Make a Dadaist Poem' (1920):

> To make a Dada poem,
>
> Take a newspaper.
>
> Take a pair of scissors.
>
> Choose an article as long as you are planning to make your poem.
>
> Cut out the article.
>
> Then cut out each of the words that make up this article and put them in a bag.
>
> Shake it gently.
>
> Then take out the scraps one after the other in the order in which they left the bag. Copy conscientiously.
>
> The poem will be like you.[87]

Three Standard Stoppages

But let us assume that Tzara's formula is not merely a misreading of *The Ego and Its Own*, nor simply an early precursor to the radical empiricism of Surrealist art: how might we reconcile this seeming discrepancy between Stirnerian theory and Dadaist practice? Here it might be instructive to consider the *3 Stoppages Etalon* by Marcel Duchamp: though Duchamp was never part of the Dadaist group, being careful, throughout his long career, to preserve his independence, Duchamp and his work can be seen to have had a profound, formative impact on Parisian Dada. It was Duchamp who introduced Stirner's book to Picabia. It was Duchamp who pioneered the *ready-mades* favoured by Dada and who remains the acknowledged master of the new medium he invented. In the course of our search for a solution to the problem outlined above we must look to Duchamp – and to the one work the artist himself later came to regard as pivotal. 'I'd say the *Three Stoppages* of 1913 is my most important work', said Duchamp, in an interview near the end of his life. 'That really was when I tapped the mainstream of my future.'[88] He explained that (while in itself *Three Standard Stoppages* is not an important work of art) it must be understood to have opened the way for him: 'the way to escape from those traditional methods of expression long associated with art'. For Duchamp the *Three Standard Stoppages* 'was a first gesture liberating [him] from the past'.[89] And in this seminal work of art we find the apparent impasse outlined above at its most pronounced. On the one hand, *Three Standard Stoppages* is the only work Duchamp himself explicitly attributed to his interest in Stirner: as Francis M. Naumann first noted in his essay 'Marcel Duchamp: a Reconciliation of Opposites' (1991), when asked in a questionnaire relating to the *Three Standard Stoppages*, issued by New York's Museum of Modern Art, to identify a specific philosopher or philosophical theory of special significance to this work, Duchamp 'cited Stirner's only major book'.[90] The piece itself, on the other hand, must disappoint those then expecting to see signs of Stirner's impact on Duchamp: as Craig Adcock remarked to Naumann, after struggling through *The Ego and Its Own*, 'I didn't see much Stirner in Duchamp … Or if you prefer, I didn't see any Duchamp in Stirner's book …'[91]

The work consists of a wooden box containing three threads each 1 metre long glued to three canvas strips and mounted on glass, together with three wooden rules carved along one edge, to match the undulating curve of the corresponding thread. Duchamp obtained these curves by holding his three threads straight and horizontal, at a height of one metre over the canvas, then letting each thread fall to the surface below, 'distorting itself *as it pleases*', thereby creating 'a new shape of the measure of length'.[92] In a short note entitled 'The Idea of the Fabrication', Duchamp explains these '3 patterns obtained in more or less similar conditions: *considered in their relation to one another* [...] are an *approximate reconstitution* of the measure of length'.[93] In fact, as Duchamp himself explains, the satirical thrust of the piece is directed at the metric system, formally inscribed on a series of platinum-iridium bars in a secure room, at a temperature just above freezing, preserved by the *Academie des Sciences* at the *Institut de France*: 'The *3 Standard Stoppages* are the meter diminished'.[94] But if that authoritative and universal system for measuring reality seems, as a great many commentators have noted, in every respect an appropriate target for egoist revolt, there remain significant disparities between Stirner's theory and Duchamp's practice that have attracted no comment since Adcock's first vaguely expressed sense of dissatisfaction and unease. In remarks such as the following, Duchamp really does seem to regard his experiment as a radical empiricism, a subjective science: 'This experiment was made in 1913 to imprison and preserve forms obtained through chance, through my chance, at the same time, the unit of length: one meter was changed from a straight line to a curved line without actually losing its identity [as] the meter, and yet casting a pataphysical doubt on the concept of a straight line as being the shortest route from one point to another'.[95] The process thus described might owe something to the scientist Henri Poincaré, or even to comedian Alfred Jarry, as is sometimes suggested, but how might one consider this a Stirnerian procedure?

I believe a clue is to be found, as Naumann first tentatively suggested, in the fact that Duchamp repeated this operation three times. 'For me the number three is important', Duchamp explains: 'one is unity, two is double, duality, and three is the rest'. Or, as he put it on another occasion, '1 a unit/2 opposition/3 a series'. 'In other words, creating a single new "meter" would only result in producing an entirely new system of measurement, with no more (or less) claim to authority than the old', writes Naumann. 'Creating three meters results in a self-sustaining system, one that does not present a simple alternative, nor a choice between two variants, but a complete system that must be comprehended and utilized in its entirety'.[96] In fact, Naumann sets out a clear distinction, consistently overlooked in subsequent scholarship on Duchamp and Dada, between 'the chance of a given individual' and the 'unique system of measurement that results'.[97] If the first acquired increasing significance for Paris Dadaists, as they embraced the Surreal, it is the latter, 'the unique system of measurement that results', which must hold our attention here. Let us be clear. Duchamp is not opposing, to an abstract system of measurement, the materiality of these three chance events (captured in patterns of thread, canvas, glass, wood); on the contrary, the *Three Standard Stoppages* is to be understood as the '*approximate reconstitution* of the measure of length' that results when those three patterns 'are *considered in their relation to one another*'.[98] Duchamp is presenting us with a physical mechanism that will permit us to *realize* (our own *unique* idea of) that immaterial and universalizing concept.

In so doing Duchamp is re-enacting the history of the metre –
and extending that history through to a logical conclusion. Unlike
Anglo-Saxon units for measuring length, the metre is not an
abstraction from the human body, but was conceived by the
Academie des Sciences as one ten-millionth of the distance *thought
to exist* between the North Pole and the Equator – and unfortunately
the planet is not a simple mathematical sphere. The metre adopted
by the Republic as the official unit of length possesses no basis in
Nature, and the struggle to realize a physical type has tested the
ingenuity of scientists ever since. The *Bureau International des
Poids et Mesures* began by producing the platinum-iridium bars
mentioned previously. But in the late nineteenth century French
physicists Michelson and Benoît recalibrated the standardized
metre in terms of the wavelength of the red line of cadmium. In
1960 the metre was officially defined by the International System
of Units as equal to 1,650,763.73 wavelengths of the orange-red
emission line in the electromagnetic spectrum of a krypton-86
atom in a vacuum. And, at present, the metre is defined as equal to
the length of the path travelled by light in a vacuum during a time
interval of 1/299,792,458 of a second.[99] The curved lines recorded
by Duchamp must reference this intense phase in the application of
wave-forms to the problem of the metre. As in the interferometer
developed by Michelson, three *etalons* (or mirrors) reflect disparate
wave-forms derived from a single source; the waves are then
recombined, to produce an *interference pattern incident* on the
retina.[100] In this new context, no one of the three standard stoppages
created by Duchamp can be regarded as a realization of the metre
and the comic inadequacy of the procedure for producing them not

a physical assault on a Stirnerian target but rather an all-important prerequisite for an *approximate reconstitution* of the measure of length *as idea*. In Stirnerian terms, the apparatus is hallowed or haunted; the device is pervaded by a *spirit* that is at no one point materially expressed.

If my interpretation is correct, what holds for this first experiment can be applied to the ready-mades that would follow. 'I wanted to get away from the physical aspect of painting', recalled Duchamp. 'I was much more interested in recreating ideas in painting.'[101] In Duchamp's view, 'Dada was an extreme protest against the physical side of painting.'[102] And, having looked at Duchamp's development of the medium, we are now in a position to understand how such a claim might be consistent with the obtrusive materiality of the ready-mades created by Dada. 'Another aspect of the "Readymade" is its lack of uniqueness... the replica of a "Readymade" delivering the same message.'[103] The version of the *Three Standard Stoppages* that is described above, for instance, is the second in a series of eight replicas produced by Arturo Schwarz in 1964, later acquired by the Tate. 'In fact nearly every one of the "Readymades" existing today is not an original in the conventional sense', remarks Duchamp.[104] The material objects he installed in art galleries of Europe and America (the birdcage, poster and urinal) were regarded by the artist as entirely disposable and interchangeable. Far from representing a recourse to materialism, the ready-made paradoxically represents the logical end point of the second phase in Stirner's teleology, towards ever greater abstraction. If the material of the past required considerable working on the part of the artist in order to express their ideas, little mediation of the material object is needed as the triumph of the spirit approaches its culmination: the total hollowing out of reality in a universal sanctification. Having begun with the transubstantiation of bread and wine through a special act of consecration performed by a priest, the holy spirit has proceeded in a series of great waves (through reformation and revolution) to that absolute limit represented by *romanticism* in philosophy and literature and plastic art: ... wherein *'Everything that lives is holy'* ... and *'The real is rational.'*[105] In the course of a talk on *The Creative Act* in 1957, Duchamp would go so far as to propose that the artist is possessed of the 'attributes of a medium', in a passage that bears a strong resemblance to Stirner on the role of the *Shaman* in the second (Mongolian) period of the world: 'through the change from inert matter into a work of art, an actual transubstantiation has taken place', states Duchamp; observing that 'To all appearances, the artist acts like a mediumistic being who, from the labyrinth beyond time and space, seeks his way out to a clearing.'[106]

But if this passage gives an accurate insight into Duchamp's own understanding of his role as an artist, how can this view (though steeped in Stirner's theory and language) be thought in any way consistent with the egoist thesis of *The Ego and Its Own*? If Duchamp's *ready-mades* are amplifying and extending, the historical progress of the spirit attacked by Stirner, how can the art of Dada be considered to encapsulate egoism? 'I know this statement will not meet with the approval of many artists who refuse this mediumistic role and insist on the validity of their own awareness in the creative act – yet, art history has consistently decided upon the virtues of a work of art through considerations completely divorced from rationalized explanations of the artist', points out Duchamp. 'In the creative act, the artist goes from intention to realization through a chain of totally subjective reactions.'[107] The result of this struggle is a difference between the intention and its realization, a difference the artist is not aware of (which is the *art coefficient*), that renders him unable to know in advance what the value of his own work will be. In Duchamp's view, the work of art is, at this moment, in a raw state – *à l'état brut* – and must be 'refined' as pure sugar from molasses – *by the spectator* – and *the digit of the coefficient* has 'no bearing whatsoever on his verdict'.[108] The artist himself is now a spectator among spectators merely with no special right to impose his own personal views on the general perception of the value of his product. In a remarkable shift from a romantic idea of the artist as culture-hero possessed of special insight into the value of his own art (together with the contempt that must then follow for the 'masses' who are not so enlightened), Duchamp would seem to be acknowledging the power of the spectator and extinction of the artist, insisting that creators must preserve themselves apart from the properties that threaten to define them: that is to say, the art itself and the status this art must then confer upon its creator, the condition of being an artist. 'The creative act takes another aspect when the spectator experiences the phenomenon of trans-mutation', says Duchamp; 'through the change from inert matter into a work of art, an actual transubstantiation has taken place, and the role of the spectator is to determine the weight of the work on the esthetic scale'. Duchamp concludes that 'All in all, the creative act is not performed by the artist alone; the spectator brings the work in contact with the external world by deciphering and interpreting its inner qualifications and thus adds his contribution to the creative act.'[109] The apparent paradox presented by Duchamp's ideas on the mediumistic or shamanic role of the artist is entirely consistent with his Stirnerian egoism because his interpretation of 'The Creative Act' as a whole is user-oriented, insisting that only the spectator (or an artist become spectator) has the potential to evaluate the transubstantiated object, to accord the artwork or sacred object some measure of *value*, through the recognition of the idea possessing that object as a property of the ego. In the following section I want to explore the political implications of this conclusion, to consider Duchamp's *theory of value* in relation to that of Marx.

Theories of value

Derrida once suggested that the spectrality of communism, in the opening lines of the *Manifesto*, might owe something to Stirner, and I would now like to suggest that the satirical analogy developed between 'fetish' and 'commodity' in *Capital* (Marx's own account of the 'prevailing stupidity') presents another striking – and significant – parallel with Stirner: his discussion of *sacred objects* in *The Ego and Its Own*.

Both Stirner and Marx are ultimately drawing on Hegel's lectures on history and religion, in which the philosopher discussed the transition from shamanism and sorcery to what is 'properly called religion' (the apprehension of an essential, Universal Being).[110] According to Hegel, religion begins with a consciousness that there is something higher than man; but in Sorcery we have not an idea of God, or of a moral faith, merely the projection of the magician's will out into the world of objective phenomena, via arbitrarily chosen objects, these being the first things that come in their way.[111] 'Just as children feel the impulse to play, and mankind the impulse to adorn themselves, there is an impulse here too to have something before one as an independent and powerful object... the consciousness of an arbitrary combination which may be just as easily broken up again, as the more precise character of that object appears at first to be of no consequence.'[112] And Hegel calls this object their *Fetish*. 'Here, in the Fetich, a kind of objective independence as contrasted with arbitrary fancies of the individual seems to manifest itself; but as the objectivity is nothing other than the fancy of the individual projecting itself into space, human individuality remains master of the image it has adopted.'[113]

Stirner collapses this important distinction between the fetish of a magician and the image of an essential, universal Being, in the course of a polemical attack on the objective idealism of the German ideology. 'The shaman and the speculative philosopher mark the bottom and top rounds on the ladder of the *inward* man, the Mongol', writes Stirner. 'Shaman and philosopher fight with ghosts, demons, *spirits*, gods.'[114] The Holy Spirit or Absolute Idea that theologians of an advanced religion like Christianity perceive in a sacred object (such as the Bible) is no less 'arbitrarily' imposed than the purely personal significance the amulet acquires in the hands of a magician. 'For him who makes to himself nothing at all out of it, it is nothing at all; for him who uses it as an amulet, it has solely the value, the significance, of a means of sorcery; for him who, like children, plays with it, it is nothing but a plaything.'[115] Of course, Stirner is not rejecting what was achieved in this progress towards the spirit; he is not advocating a recourse to that primitive mastery human individuality is thought to have maintained over the fetish-object in sorcery. On the contrary, Stirner receives with thanks what centuries of culture have acquired for him, and is not prepared simply to throw over things of the spirit. 'Without a doubt culture has made me *powerful*', he acknowledges; 'I know, and have gained the force for it by culture, that I need not let myself be coerced by any of my appetites, pleasures, emotions, etc.; I am their – *master*; in like manner I become, through the sciences and arts, the *master* of the refractory world, whom sea and earth obey, and to whom even the stars must give an account of themselves.'[116] The spirit made him master of the world, but now Stirner must master the spirit too or be mastered by it, and he will achieve this by a continual consumption of that which is his *own*. ' "Absolute thinking" is that which forgets that it is *my* thinking, that *I* think, and that it exists only through *me*', he writes. 'But I, as I, swallow up again what is mine, am its master; it is only my *opinion*, which I can at any moment *change*, annihilate, take back into myself, and consume.'[117]

Marx's famous chapter on the 'fetishism of the commodity' presents compelling parallels with this subversion of Hegel on sorcery, and the profound differences between the two theories emerge all the more starkly as a result. Appearing at first an 'extremely obvious, trivial thing', analysis of the commodity brings out that it is a 'strange thing, abounding in metaphysical subtleties and theological niceties'.[118] In a passage that anticipates Duchamp's thoughts on the substantial transmutation the art-object seems to undergo, beyond any physical adjustment performed by the artist, the philosopher argues that the transformation of wood into a table involves a change that transcends sensuousness as soon as it emerges as commodity. 'It not only stands with its feet on the ground, but, in relation to all other commodities, it stands on its head, and evolves out of its wooden brain grotesque ideas, far more wonderful than if it were to begin dancing of its own free will.'[119] In order to find analogies Marx must take flight into the misty realms of religion described by Hegel. 'There the products of the human brain appear as autonomous figures endowed with a life of their own, which enter into relations both with each other and with the human race', he observes. 'So it is in the world of commodities with the products of men's hands.' Marx calls this 'the fetishism that attaches itself to the product of labour as soon as they are produced as commodities'.[120] As in Stirner decades earlier, anthropological imagery derived from Hegel is used (playfully) to illustrate the semblance of objectivity possessed by the commodity-form. But where Stirner might have attributed these mystical properties to the labour of the individual craftsman, Marx is perfectly clear that only the use-value acquired by a commodity is the product of human labour, and there is nothing mysterious about that.[121] Whence, then, arises the enigmatic character of the product of labour, as soon as it assumes the commodity-form? 'Objects of utility become commodities only because they are the products of the labour of private individuals who work independently of each other', explains Marx. 'Since the producers do not come into social contact until they exchange the products of their labour, the specific social characteristics of their private labours appear only within this exchange.'[122] The result is that, to the producers, social relations between their private labours appear not as social relations between persons in their work, but as social relations between material things possessed of a uniform objectivity as *value*. 'Later on, men try to decipher the hieroglyphic, to get behind the secret of their own social product', writes Marx.[123] 'The belated scientific discovery that the products of labour, in so far as they are values, are merely the material expressions of the human labour expended to produce them, marks an epoch in the history of mankind's development, but by no means banishes the semblance of objectivity possessed by the social characteristics of labour.'[124] We are thus led to conclude that Stirner's recognition of alienated personal properties in an artefact's apparently objective value will make no change at all. Marx closes by remarking drily that:

> Something which is only valid for this particular form of production, the production of commodities, namely the fact that the specific social character of private labours carried on independently of each other consists in their equality as human labour, and, in the product, assumes the form of the existence of value, appears to those caught up in the relations of commodity production (and this is true both before and after the above-mentioned scientific discovery) to be just as ultimately valid as the fact that the scientific dissection of the air into its component parts left the atmosphere itself unaltered in its physical configuration.[125]

Situated within this new context Duchamp's essay 'The Creative Artist' emerges as the obvious Stirnerian riposte – accepting Marxist 'reification' but refusing the reorganization of social relations that theory must seem to require. As is implied by Stirner, a theoretically rigorous and consistent egoism cannot rest content with recognizing only the private labour that has gone into making the artefact, but must also requisition the objective idea that centuries of culture have acquired for him: the uniform objectivity of a value or measurement system that emerges in the course of social exchange. The subjective nature of value first noted by Marx is acknowledged: and becomes the basis for a theory of value that identifies the private enterprise involved in the exchange (rather than the private labour preliminary to that exchange) as the true generator of value and measure. Working independently and from a very different starting-point, Duchamp has in fact arrived at the foundational insight of what is now called the Austrian School, the "radical subjectivist" or "neo-liberal" approach to economic theory pioneered by Carl Menger in his *Grundsätze de Volkswirtschaftslehre* (1871) that informed the economic policy of politicians such as Margaret Thatcher, Ronald Reagan and Alan Greenspan. 'Just as a penetrating investigation of mental processes makes the cognition of external things appear to be merely our consciousness of the impressions made by the external things upon our persons, and thus, in the final analysis, merely the cognition of states of our own persons, so too, in the final analysis, is the importance that we attribute to things of the external world only an outflow of the importance to us of our continued existence and development (life and well-being)', writes Menger. 'The measure of value is entirely subjective in nature, and for this reason a good can have great value to one economising individual, little value to another, and no value at all to a third, depending upon the differences in their requirements and available amounts.'[126] Engels is wrong then in saying that 'This egoism is simply the essence of present society and present man brought to consciousness…' In fact, the logic underpinning egoist Dada is not that of classic or liberal economics, but that of neoliberal economics. In this light the extraordinary reception history of Dada in Paris and New York need not appear so surprising. The ultimate that can be said against Marxist theory is not – or is not primarily – the culmination of all the theory intrinsic to the nineteenth century, but is entirely at one, on this fundamental point, with the radical economic theory that has become the basis for our own 'prevailing stupidity'.[127]

Duchamp was the father of conceptual art, and the theoretical position outlined in the previous paragraph has had an enduring impact following the reappraisal of that artist's oeuvre and the Dadaism with which he was loosely associated in the sixties. (In this the Pop Artist Richard Hamilton played a key role, having undertaken the restoration and reproduction of Duchamp's *The Bride Stripped Bare of Her Bachelors, Even* (1915–1923) and the accompanying notes, published in the *White Box* of 1967). Having come so far we are in a position to understand how *ready-mades* produced by Young British Artists of the nineties (for instance) might constitute daring insurrectionary art even though they were favoured and promoted by multi-millionaire Tory strategist Charles Saatchi. Neither co-opted nor proven to be ineffectual, the latest wave of conceptual art has simply shared from the start their patron's (quite radical) theoretical assumptions concerning the creation of value. Like Duchamp's *Three Standard Stoppages*, Damien Hirst's *For the Love of God* (2007) is nothing less than an object-lesson in Mengerian economics. First exhibited at the White Cube Gallery in London and costing £14 million to produce, the piece consists of a platinum cast of a skull (with real teeth) that has been encrusted with

8,601 diamonds: a substance Menger singled out as a stumbling block for classically trained liberal economists and for Marxist theorists alike – at once having rather less use value than a glass of water, and possessing an exchange value demonstrably unrelated to the labour cost and 'other goods' applied in bringing it to market. 'Whether a diamond was found accidentally or was obtained from a diamond pit with the employment of a thousand days of labor is completely irrelevant for its value', observes Menger. 'The quantities of labor or of other means of production applied to its production cannot, therefore, be the determining factor in the value of a good.'[128] Hirst himself underscores the uncertainty surrounding the inherent worth of diamond in publicity material that often accompanies the piece: 'just a bit of glass, with accumulated metaphorical significance? Or genuine objects of supreme beauty connected with life?'[129] It is certainly telling that most of the press coverage and criticism relating to the piece is fixated on the cost of production and price tag. *For the Love of God* is rumoured to have been sold to an anonymous consortium for £50 million, and there has been feverish speculation ever since that the artist has not in fact found a buyer for the work, or that he purchased the piece himself, part of a marketing strategy that ought to bring about a re-evaluation of the Hirst 'brand'.

Before closing, I would like to suggest, briefly, that the legacy of Duchamp's egoist art must raise serious questions concerning the economic logic that has provided the basis for the reinvention of Western society since the late seventies. In short, there is a tension within this theory of value – between the radically subjectivist principle that constitutes its foundation and the manipulation of measurement systems on the part of an elite which renders value for

most people an objective factor over which they have no sort of say –
that is developing into an outright contradiction. Duchamp thought
that everyone can play a part in the production of value: in a recent
Reith Lecture, the artists Grayson Perry acknowledges that certain
people are certainly in a rather better position to pronounce upon this
than the rest. 'It will be peers, serious critics and collectors, dealers,
curators and then the public', explains Perry. 'And this validation
process is I think, I mean I like to think, I don't know if I'm right
in this, I like to think it's self-correcting to a certain extent.'[130] In a
response published in *The Guardian* in 2014, novelist Will Self is not
so sure: 'Public galleries have often accepted artworks as donations,
but in the 1990s they began accepting such donations from the
artists themselves, and then putting them on display', he writes.
'This represented a flagrant disregard for curatorial standards, and
registered the exact point at which the hyper-rich artists and their
still more moneyed dealers began to call the tune – henceforth the
"crap" silting up public galleries would be deposited there by the ebb
and flow of finance.'[131]

The Barrès trial

On 13 May 1921, Parisian Dada gathered at the Salle des Sociétés
Savantes, and became a revolutionary tribunal. At the instigation
of André Breton, writer and politician Maurice Barrès was to
be charged, by prosecutor Georges Ribemont Dessaignes, with
attacking the security of spirit, having apparently relinquished his
early enthusiasm for Stirnerian egoism, expressed in inspirational

writing such as *Le Culte du Moi* (1910), in order to embrace a series of political causes that privilege class, nationality, race and religion over individuality: Boulangist, federalist, nationalist, anti-Semite, fascist and finally parliamentary conservative. The Dadaists assembled in the robes and horse-hair wigs proper to the persons of a law court, and (with a dummy standing in for the absent accused) proceeded to play out this show trial in Wonderland. The moment is often thought to mark a turning point for the French avant-garde, part of a programme of events that paved the way for Breton's decisive break with Dadaism the following year and the launch of Surrealism – and as a result the political significance of this trial has attracted considerable critical attention, with critics scouring the transcript for clues that might explain the nature of this key transition within the modern movement. Undoubtedly, the trial does reflect a further fracturing of the residual French anarchist community, as Stirnerian egoists increasingly moved to defined political positions on the Left and Right: that is to say, towards communism and fascism (via Nietzsche). But having come so far we are now in a position to see that Breton's objective was not, or not primarily, to punish what many Stirnerian egoists were becoming in the interwar Republic, but to interrogate the political implications of Stirner's great refusal. 'The problem was to determine the extent to which a man could be held accountable if his will to power led him to champion conformist values that are diametrically opposed the ideas of his youth', Breton explained. 'If there was a betrayal, what were the stakes? And what recourse did one have against them? Above and beyond the Barrès case, these questions were to agitate surrealism for quite some time ...'[132]

Breton had hoped to prove that Stirnerian egoists cannot be
trusted to guarantee that their present activity is not going to
be undermined by their future activities. 'Not only has Barrès
[for instance] found himself invested in a mandate he has not carried
out', claims Breton, 'but the particularly brilliant situation in which
he places himself, joined to the action that...carries on the works
whose republication he continually authorises...shed doubt on the
value of all revolutionary agitation'. In fact evidence produced during
the trial would present another, altogether more shocking, possibility.
On being asked if he could promise that he would not in the future
undertake such an 'attack on the spirit', Tzara would reply:

> I am certainly the man in the best position to see everything
> that might happen. I change only my opinion and every delay in
> each change makes me just that much more keen to disappear.
> I'm not saying that I will not become a nationalist, but I am sure
> all my friends know that it is in a different spirit from the low
> demagoguery of the accused.[133]

But then how could one not in the best position to see into Tzara's
soul ever know that a betrayal of the egoist principle had not taken
place? Might not Barrès himself, even up to that point, have remained
faithful to the Stirnerian egoism expressed in the early writing that
the Dadaists admired so much? Had there, in fact, been no betrayal,
no lost leader? The philosophy that had provided the single most
important theoretical foundation for Paris Dada is shown to be
compatible with (perhaps the driving force behind) a long public
career in far-right politics. This is an outcome that Breton had not,
one senses, apparently anticipated: and he would later reflect bitterly

that 'It is just because Tzara, who had eyes for no one, one idle day took it into his head to have [eyes] for himself, which means that in the short term he already seems no more than a run-of-the-mill general of the Republic who turned coat and whom suicide awaits on some mistress's grave.'[134] In closing, I would like to suggest that, in this insight emerging from a trial that effectively marked the end of Parisian Dada, we have a clue to the great problem within Stirnerian egoism, which was to re-surface within the Anglo-American writing considered in the following chapters. Persisting with the once popular Stirnerian paradigm into the interwar year, writers such as Dora Marsden, James Joyce and Wyndham Lewis can be seen to struggle with a contradiction inherent to a philosophy that must negate everything, in a perpetual and all-encompassing analysis, for an end that must remain one's own.

2

PHILOSOPHIC ALGEBRA
Dora Marsden's Lingual Psychology

T.S. Eliot eventually came to regret writing his most famous essay 'Tradition and the Individual Talent'. While not repudiating the piece, Eliot thought it a product of immaturity: 'That, the best known of my essays, appeared in 1917, when I had taken over the assistant-editorship of *The Egoist* on Richard Aldington's being called up for military service, and before I had been asked to contribute to any other periodical.'[1] But just as the new (the really new) work of art acquires a spot in that ideal order formed by the existing monuments, so Eliot's critical effort now persists in a context entirely removed from the conditions of its production. 'The emotion of art is impersonal', concludes Eliot – and this claim has had a profound impact not merely upon how his poetry has been read over the years but on how we continue to interpret the phase of Modernist innovation in which he participated.[2] Across the arts, Modernism has been seen typically to require the 'continual surrender' of individual subjects to something 'more valuable', a systematic totality that might be a vision of culture or race or religion, a political ideology or pattern in history, an architectural theory or new model of the mind. In each case, Modernists were participating in a dissolution of the individual subject into its component parts, its physical, psychological and sociological functions. 'The point of view which I am struggling to attack', Eliot writes, 'is perhaps related to the metaphysical theory of the substantial unity of the soul'.[3] The extent to which the argument advanced in 'Tradition and the Individual Talent' still continues to shape perceptions of Modernism cannot be overstated. Any self-professed post-modernist will say that the subordination of individuals to authority is the defining characteristic of whatever Modernism they happen to be rejecting; their emphasis on the individual subject is inevitably the precise point on which they have taken issue with their totalizing predecessors.

But what to make of the curious fact that Eliot's Impersonal Manifesto appeared in *The Egoist: An Individualist Review*? Or the fact that Eliot began his career as a writer with the publication of this glowing review of the book that introduced Stirnerian egoism to the English-speaking world? 'Now that Arthur Symons is no longer active in English letters, Mr James Huneker alone represents modernity in criticism', states Eliot in a review of Huneker's book in *The Harvard Advocate* (1909). 'The Egoists are all men – French and German – of highly individual, some of perverse and lunary, genius.'[4] I would suggest that Eliot's unease in later years with 'Tradition and the Individual Talent' must relate, not to the premises set out in that essay (this aesthetic of self-renunciation would in fact provide the basis for his subsequent projects), but to the circumstances in which that essay was produced. His preface from 1963 (quoted above) stresses the occasional, circumstantial nature of the piece. No complete meaning alone – but significance in its relation to the philosophical standpoint of a magazine that was by then long since forgotten.

Formerly called *The New Freewoman*, the journal was renamed *The Egoist* on 1 January 1914, ostensibly in response to a letter sent by poet Ezra Pound (among others) to the two editors Dora Marsden and Harriet Shaw Weaver, and calling for them to adopt a 'title which will mark the character of your paper as an organ of individualists of both sexes, of the individualist principle in every department of life'.[5] This moment has been viewed by many ever since as tantamount to a coup whereby male Modernists secured a platform for their literary experiments at the expense of a publication dedicated to the cause of women's cultural and political expression. In fact, the truth is rather more complicated. The founding editor of the magazine, Dora Marsden, had been expressing disenchantment with the Pankhursts and the Suffragette Cause for months, and had been setting out the possibilities of a radical individualism based upon the egoism of Max Stirner. Far from having experimental pieces by young writers such as James Joyce, H.D., William Carlos Williams, D.H. Lawrence and T.S. Eliot imposed on her by Pound, Marsden very much remained the moving spirit at *The Egoist* after the rebrand. As Bruce Clarke has demonstrated, in a ground-breaking study of the role played by Marsden in this formative period in English-language Modernism, Marsden hoped that her new writers might eventually forge an aesthetic that would build upon the radical implications of an egoist philosophy. This is the philosophy that Eliot is responding to in his (satirical?) essay 'Tradition and the Individual Talent'.

Modernist egoism has received a fraction of the attention
devoted to variations on the Impersonal Theory of Modernism. As
noted above, Clarke has written an excellent revisionist account
of Marsden's role as an editor, but as John F. Welsh has observed,
too little of it is concerned with Marsden's interpretation of egoist
thought. 'Most of the literature on Marsden is concerned with her
role in the history of feminism and her place in early modernist
literature.'[6] In his own book, Welsh traces the impact of that
Stirnerian philosophy upon Marsden's work but repeats the mistake
that Clarke corrected when he insists there is no connection between
Marsden's concerns and those of the young Anglo-American
Modernists her journal helped to promote.[7] In this essay I show that
this failure to appreciate the extent of the impact Marsden's writing
had on English-language Modernism is a mistake. As critic Michael
Levenson once noted, individualism is a crucial element in the
foundational moment of English-language Modernism: and (unlike
Levenson), I believe that Marsden's inventive interpretation of
Stirnerian egoism can be seen to persist, a presence even within the
later authoritarian Modernisms.[8] If this is not widely recognized,
this is because Stirnerian egoism has not yet been fully interrogated
and understood, its necessary implications taken into account.

The egoist

Friedrich Nietzsche might have been a Stirnerian egoist – but only
for a fortnight in October 1865. Two independent studies have
recently found that Dr Eduard Mushacke, father of Nietzsche's

fellow student Hermann Mushacke, had been a personal friend of Stirner, a man referred to in Mackay's biography as 'Mussak'. The young Nietzsche arrived in Berlin, fired with enthusiasm for the 'lively spirit' of the Forties, eager to learn from this veteran, 'The old Mushacke...the most loveable man I ever met'.[9] It is probable that it was in the course of this visit that Nietzsche encountered the philosopher with whom he would later confess a spiritual kinship.[10] But the sense of solidarity brought about by his brief moment of interest in Stirner hardly amounts to more than that. The subsequent crisis that initiated Nietzsche's evolution into a philosopher would be brought about by that 'dark genius' Schopenhauer, whose work he would discover before the month was out in a second-hand bookstall in Leipzig. Nor could Stirner have helped Nietzsche much in his rebellion against Schopenhauer, decades later, following his break with Wagner and Bayreuth: the tactics of the iconoclast being applied in each case to such radically different targets as Hegelian idealism upon the one hand and Schopenhauer's reworking of the empirical tradition of philosophy on the other.

In spite of this, Nietzsche's reported fear that he might be accused of plagiarizing the earlier philosopher was to be realized soon after his collapse into mental and physical paralysis in 1889.[11] Eduard von Hartmann claimed that being 'beyond good and evil' was by no means a new idea, since it had already been presented by Max Stirner: 'in a masterful fashion, and with a clearness and frankness, that leaves nothing to be desired'.[12] Nietzsche's family and friends rallied to defend him against the charges. And so began an intense and inconclusive argument lasting twenty years over the extent to which

Superman was the Son of Egoist. This futile controversy necessitated republication, and so, forty years after being forgotten, *Der Einzige und sein Eigentum* returned with a reputation greater and more evil, if possible, than ever before. The biography by Mackay was published in 1893. Two translations into French followed in 1900. There were further translations into Italian, Russian and Danish. And then, in the United States, James L. Walker, a Texas newspaperman, began to write about egoism in the pages of Benjamin Tucker's anarchist weekly *Liberty*. In collaboration with Emma Heller and Steven T. Byington, Walker produced a translation into English that would appear, four years after his death, in an edition published by Tucker in New York in 1907, with a second edition published in London and New York in 1913. And the culmination to this untimely, second surge to celebrity would come that same year when Dora Marsden, editor of *The New Freewoman*, would propose in the final edition of that paper to change the title on 1 January 1914 to *The Egoist*.

In her editorial, Marsden noted that this reflected a change in emphasis that had taken place some time earlier. 'Our own dissatisfaction with the title [*The New Freewoman*] is due to the fact that it fails to suggest itself for what it is', she insists. 'The critic who accuses us of selling "Aeolian harps under the name of tin whistles" indicates the positive element from which the paper suffers.'[13] In fact, Marsden's interest in egoism can be traced right back to material she produced, not for *The New Freewoman*, but its earlier incarnation, *The Freewoman*, in 1911.

That paper had been founded in a spirit of disenchantment with the Suffragette Movement in which Marsden had played such a leading part. In a piece entitled 'Bondwomen', in the first issue,

Marsden presented a distinction that anticipated her interest in Stirnerian insurrection, distinguishing between women who are happy to retain a 'permanently subordinate position' and freewomen who reject every form of domination, including the democratic state, in the belief that only their own personal resources can effect their liberation as individuals.[14] Marsden was drawing upon personal insights gained in the course of her own campaign of guerrilla protest, performed in the name of Pankhurst's Women's Social and Political Union, but often initiated without the prior approval of that organization. Marsden had been propelled into the limelight in 1909, following her arrest on trying to break through an early police 'kettle'. She had initiated the hunger strikes, endured the force-feeding that became such a rallying tool for the campaign for Women's Votes, and, most famously, Marsden had found a means to circumvent tight security arrangements put in place about Empire Hall in Southport, in order to heckle Winston Churchill, Liberal Home Secretary, from the skylight on 4 December 1904. Marsden felt, justly, that her form of direct action had achieved more for the Cause than the cautious approach adopted by the WSPU. The praise she received from leading Suffragettes after the event must have reinforced this belief. Yet each action had involved Marsden in a struggle not merely against the political authorities but against autocrats within her own organization. From the moment of her resignation from WSPU, following a series of attempts to curtail her freedom of action, Marsden had been actively seeking a new theoretical basis for insurrection and self-liberation. A year after founding *The Freewoman* it became increasingly clear to her readers that she had found this in Stirner.

On 8 August 1912, in an article entitled 'The Growing Ego',
Marsden remarked the 'penetrative influence' that *The Ego and Its
Own* had recently acquired over *The Freewoman*, and sought to put
clear water between them. While accepting the truth of Stirner's
book, she insists that, though concepts such as ethics are indeed
phantasmal and neither postulate nor control the ego, Stirner
had failed to recognize that if the ego requires 'realization of itself
in morality, or religion, or God, then by virtue of the ego and its
own supremacy, the realization will be forthcoming'.[15] Marden's
first reference to Stirner also indicates her divergence from his
philosophy, on a point upon which she would later elaborate at
length. But having once established the nature of this fundamental
difference to her own satisfaction, Marsden's praise is less qualified.
In *The New Freewoman*, just a little over a year later, Marsden hails
The Ego and His Own as 'the most powerful work that has ever
emerged from a human mind'.[16] And a few months after that, in
January 1914, Marsden assures critics that she is perfectly relaxed
about being mistaken for a Stirnerian egoist, although 'Stinerian' is
not the adjective most fittingly applied to the egoism of *The Egoist*. 'If
our beer bears a resemblance in flavour to other brands, it is due to
the similarity of taste in the makers', explains Marsden.

> Having said this, we do not seek to minimize the amount of
> Stirner which may be traced herein. The contrary rather, since
> having no fear that creative genius folded its wings when Stirner
> laid down his pen, we would gladly credit to him – unlike so many
> of the individualists who have enriched themselves somewhat at
> his hands – the full measure of his astounding creativeness.[17]

The politics of egoism

The New Freewoman would represent the concerted attempt on Marsden's part to apply her highly individual interpretation of Stirnerian egoism to every aspect of contemporary culture. 'Liberty, Equality, Fraternity, Unity, Justice, Truth, Humanity, Law, Mumbo-Jumbo, Mesopotamia, Abracadabra' – Marden's editorial rejects them all as 'Empty Concept', as 'futile products of men pursuing their own shadow'. Marsden explains that 'An intellectual concept is not, strictly speaking, a concept at all: it represents the giving of a "local habitation and a name" to a "Nothing".'[18] In later years Marsden would come to realize that nothing less than a complete overhaul of the language was required, 'Our war is with words and in their every aspect', she writes: 'grammar, accidence, syntax: body, blood and bone'.[19] As might be expected, 'The Woman Movement' is among the first singled out for destruction, along with Freedom, Liberty and the rest. 'Accurately speaking,' writes Marsden, 'there *is* no "Woman Movement". "Woman" is doing nothing – she has, indeed, no existence.'[20] In Marsden's view, individual women should begin to assess what they actually want, rather than subordinating their desires to class or sex or race or state, 'or any other faked-up authority'. Any description by function is necessarily reductive because: 'The centre of the Universe lies in the desire of the Individual, and the Universe for the individual has no meaning apart from their individual satisfactions, a means to an end.'[21] In a phrase that bears a striking resemblance to British prime minister Thatcher's reformulation of the egoist programme, Marsden insists that 'There *is* no corporate life. There are only individuals'.[22] 'Society' is a mere collection of individuals – that and nothing more. '[The] so-called Wholes are nothing whatsoever – mere verbalities, and […] in sacrificing the one to the other the Real is destroyed in the interests of the Unreal, the Living sacrificed to the Non-existent.'[23] Yet, historically, to this point, this is always what has happened: 'the self is the culprit; therefore the self must be put into bondage, restricted in its power to do mischief', concludes Marsden, in the final number of *The New Freewoman*. 'The states, the churches, laws, moral codes, duties, conventions, public opinion are the variant forms which the efforts to put the self under restraint have taken.'[24]

As Marsden noted, the effect of much in *The New Freewoman* upon its earliest supporters was – as 'disconcerting as a blow struck upon the face of a child'.[25] One American correspondent, for instance, complained that 'my simple Middle Western intelligence is inadequate to grasp the import of a paper so post-everything as *The New Freewoman*'.[26] In fact, Marsden's rigorous interpretation of Stirnerian egoism had taken her to a political position far beyond what even that philosopher's advocates had been prepared to accept. In March 1914 Benjamin Tucker, Stirner's English-language publisher, and former supporter of the journal, informed Marsden that she was not an anarchist – but an 'Egoist and Archist', noting sourly that this unfortunate combination had already figured largely in the world's history.[27]

In a series of arguments conducted across the correspondence and editorial sections of *The New Freewoman* and *The Egoist*, Marsden would take Tucker and Byington to task for failing to understand the full implications of Stirnerian egoism. Like the socialists of the previous century, these anarchists are accused of holding fast to an oppressive humanism, 'humanitarian fallacies'.[28] 'Such an one as does not hold in awe the Rights of Man, who does not bow down to the worth of Man as Man, and not merely as a living being, and hold it Sacred and Holy, he shall be held to be not of the community of Man but a monster preying upon the human fold, fit only to be flung out ...'[29] Like Stirner, Marsden accuses former comrades of being insufficiently separated from the devout: 'They belong to the Christians' Church and should be recognized as Christianity's picked children.'[30] In expecting free individuals to adhere to their moral code, to respect the rights of others after any external compulsion to do so had been eliminated, anarchists were preparing a more subtle, more tyrannical power of repression than any that the world had yet known: 'as compared with the power of egoistic repression the Ego comes up against in an ordinary "State", that which it meets in the shape of Conscience is infinitely more oppressive and searching.'[31] Should the anarchist ever effect his revolution the extent to which his code represented the imposition of his own individual will upon an unwilling populace would soon become immediately clear. 'On the morrow of his successful revolution he would need to set about finding means to protect his "anarchistic" notions: and would find himself protecting his own interests with all the powers he could command, like a vulgar Archist [that is to say, a Leader]: formulating his Laws and maintaining his State, until some franker Archist arrived to displace and supercede him.'[32]

Tucker's use of the term 'Egoist' as an insult indicates the extent to which Marsden had succeeded in persuading this early advocate of Stirner that he had been very wrong to think the philosophy compatible with more humanitarian forms of anarchist revolt. Marsden had emerged as the sole committed exponent of Stirnerian insurrection over Revolution. As Welsh has noted, 'Her egoism is a pure critique of the extant society that does not envision any specific transformation or any concept of reconstructed social life.'[33] The process of self-liberation is presented as an ongoing struggle regardless of the social formation confronting the egoist: because coercion is simply another name for the world that humans inhabit. 'The implication of Marsden's egoism is that coercion and predation are universalized in human relationships', concludes Welsh. 'Social life can be little more than the war of each against all.'[34] The later transition from individualism to franker forms of Archism on the part of many Modernists must seem less surprising once the extent to which individualism in this period meant Stirnerian egoism is recognized.

Marsden has continued to attract strong criticism for betraying and undermining political, economic and cultural empowerment of women. In *Pink Guitar* (1990) poet and essayist Rachel Blau Du-Plessis – one of the few critics to perceive that the journal's ideological shift to egoism was driven by Marsden – offers a devastating appraisal. 'How wonderful to be able to editorialize that the debates on gender were over, that women "can be as 'free' now as they have the power to be", that the assertion of freewoman status no longer need happen, that indeed, such assertions were divisive, backward looking, a form of protectionism, and were not modern'.[35] Recalling certain criticisms levelled at Stirner by Marx and Engels, Du-Plessis argues that 'the assertion of Self in Singularity that the new title claimed was a myth of – let us speak in shorthand – false consciousness. It did not ask how "ego" was socially formed, in what conjunctures'.[36] This reading is seconded by Bruce Clarke: in defining ego as ontologically primary and existentially fluid, Marsden could never acknowledge the extent to which the ego is a secondary effect in which ideological structures persist; is a contingent precipitate of a fixating identification, some introjected ego-ideal. 'From her first feminisms to her later egoisms', Clarke concludes, 'Dora Marsden remained a phenomenological idealist'.[37]

But this is to overlook the extent to which egoism emerges precisely through Marsden's deconstruction of pre-existing ideological categories: the normative gender-theories and the humanist political ideologies that constituted left-wing political discourse in Edwardian England. Marsden's refusal to subordinate individual contingency to categorical imperatives of Woman and Motherhood might be said to have anticipated the approach of more recent gender theorists, such as Judith Butler, who have questioned the essentialism and the resulting push to conformity inherent to earlier versions of feminism. Marsden was not, initially at least, committed to an idea, but rather to the destruction of every idea; her philosophy was not a philosophy but methodology; not a system of thought – egoism is process, ongoing negation, a procedure for critical thinking. The egoist is analyst.

A Lingual Psychology

In the first issue of 1915 Marsden would begin to apply this methodology to 'all the debatable and insoluble problems in philosophy'.[38] Having dealt with ideas underpinning feminism and anarchism to her own satisfaction, Marsden would carry her war against 'The Word' right into the heart of the 'verbal chaos' produced by philosophers, over the past 3,000 years, in the field of epistemology. 'Philosophy is doomed to sterility as long as it is based upon unapprehended words and acknowledged enigmas which keep its activities widely divided from the currents of vital interests', she declared. 'The knots have been born of the form of the questions and have been unwittingly placed there by the very species of enquirers who later become so puzzled to find out its significance.'[39] In a series of four essays entitled 'I Am' and 'Truth and Reality I-III', Marsden would bring all 'grammatical forms' that confuse theories of knowledge under a 'psychological scalpel'; and from July 1916 she would commit her journal to this 'unique and supremely important task', pursuing her conviction that 'analysis' is 'philosophic method' through a single, singularly ambitious, series of articles called 'Lingual Psychology' or 'The Science of Signs' that ran right on through to the termination of *The Egoist* in December 1919.[40] 'Philosophy', claims Marsden, 'is the watchdog, censor, guardian, of the universal symbolising activity; but because the only comprehensive system of symbols is language, and since every other variety of symbol in exact proportion to its genuineness and intelligibility will debouch into speech and express its specialised function in speech-terms, it has been thought fitting to describe the new philosophy as "Lingual Psychology"'.[41] The egoistical theory underpinning Marsden's analytical practice thus emerges from her critical reading of the great modern debate between phenomenological idealism and psychological empiricism.

Her theory presents a singular mixture of the two, reconciling these competing perspectives in a manner that bears comparison with many of the other hybrid philosophies to appear in Europe during this era. Marsden follows Berkeley in believing that *esse est percipi*. Nothing exists that is not perceived – perceived, not as an idea, as in Berkeley, but as sensation, or, as Marsden sometimes puts it, as experienced emotion. Like Schopenhauer, Marsden recognizes that ego is self-aware through physical intuition: 'Thinking widens the limits of knowledge, but the base of the latter is in feeling.'[42] If we accept there is such a thing as an idea, this can only be a second order of physical sensibility:

[T]he matter of intellect', she writes, 'so much debated, [is] likely to prove no matter at all, to be merged and explained in the tale of the emotions; likely to be proved that it is instinct, well served by senses; so well served that it is in the way to forget its origin and meaning; that the senses are attenuated feeling, filaments of the soul-stuff drawn fine, told off from the deeper-seated well of life to stand on sentinel duty at the periphery; their attention turned outward; placed mainly in the head because the head goes first, cautious, expanding little emotion until sure of the surroundings; the intenser vitalized life of soul trailing behind; the senses occupied with the environment, their attention monopolized by that; the deeper reaches of emotion busy with the organizing personality, kneading memory, the record of the buffeting of experience into the permanence of the individual ego'.[43]

The first intimations of this extraordinary synthesis can be traced right back to a passage written to mark the reinvention of *The New Freewoman* as the journal for philosophic inquiry and poetic experiment in 1914. 'If we could get into the habit of describing a man', Marsden writes, 'as he feels himself, instead of the physical image under which he presents himself to sight [...] If we described him – as an artist would – that is, as he feels himself, we should say an intense flaming heart of sensitiveness in a sheath of material substance, in and out of which it can send piercing fingers, keen tongues of itself as foragers [...]'.[44] This is the human soul. Not a thought. Nothing to do with thought. But a 'thing' – 'as electricity running along a wire is a thing'.[45] In language that anticipates Virginia Woolf's famous vision of Mrs Brown in a railway carriage, Marsden projects a subjective and vital image of experience that seems to affirm the importance of the Stirnerian principle of maintaining ego in a state of creative flux. As Clarke observes in connection with this passage, 'the goal of life in any individual manifestation, in any ego, is to fend off fixating forces and maintain itself in pure onward motion'.[46]

Schopenhauer had introduced physical intuition merely by way of a supplement to the phenomenological idealism of Kant: a means of engaging with the *Ding an sich*. But Marsden entirely rejects a Kantian distinction between appearance and reality. According to Marsden, 'The conundrum of "Thing-in-itself" could be put thus: "What do we feel when we don't?" or, "What is there felt we don't feel?" or, "What is there when there isn't?"'.[47] In this respect, her position might be thought to resemble that of the English phenomenologist F.H. Bradley. In a passage later reproduced in Eliot's 'Notes' to *The Waste Land*, Bradley had once written that

My external sensations are no less private to myself than are my thoughts and feelings. In either case my experience falls within my own circle, a circle closed on the outside; and, with all its elements alike, every sphere is opaque to the others which surround it…In brief, regarded as an existence which appears in a soul, the whole world for each is peculiar and private to that soul.[48]

But Bradley and Eliot were (elsewhere) careful to maintain the distinction between these closed circles of experience and an individual soul. This is not a possibility that Marsden investigates: and so her 'ego-universe' (which Bradley called 'experience' – and not '*my* experience') is never exposed to the rigorous analysis that Marsden reserves for empiricist psychology on the one hand and for phenomenological idealism on the other. The 'real' world and the world of thought are collapsed, but the resulting amalgam (the possibility of its discontinuity with the ego) is not interrogated. 'The total thus presented by my body, and my external world, I call my universe or ego', concludes Marsden. '[Ego] is the comprehensive description of the entire structure of feeling.'[49]

In fact, Marsden's views present strong affinities with that '*theoretical egoism*' that Schopenhauer had cautioned readers against: for which 'Scenes, sounds, smells, tastes, color, shape, size, space, time, stress, strain, are merely aspects of the "I"'.[50] Like Schopenhauer's hypothetical solipsist, Marsden was not prepared to recognize that there could be a 'world' outside the 'ego': 'that which we call the objective world are but so many patterns and chords – auras – thrown out by the "I" itself'.[51] Marsden avoids outright scepticism (or insanity) by suggesting (like Bradley before her) that if certain objects perceived in her projected world appear to be themselves projecting a world, it is only logical to assume they are in fact doing so: as there is no longer any distinction between the appearance and reality. 'The difference between my "World"', she writes, 'and this plant's "World" is a difference not in "a" World common to us both, but between me and the plant. Our worlds? We each grow our own!'[52] To be alive is precisely to grow a world, to be an ego experiencing 'the whole gallery of images which it can throw out from itself', and this remains the case 'whether "I" be a tree, or a worm, or a reader of "The Egoist"'.[53]

In fact, the only difference between a human ego and that of an animal would seem to consist in the much greater capacity of the former (result of a unique configuration of tongue and hand) to 'change its present World into a fuller and more definite world'.[54] In her 'Lingual Psychology', Marsden would elaborate on this point, postulating a division within the human ego of outer 'sensation' and inner 'conception' or 'idea' – 'which could forthwith be translated as Vital and Verbal respectively'.[55] That is to say, Marsden reiterates the Kantian distinction between the *noumenal* and the *phenomenal* (i.e. reality or the Thing-in-itself and appearance) *within* what Kant would have designated the latter: within the total feeling of the Subject. According to Marsden, sensation is *spatial* and *substantial*, 'A thing is the effect of movements generated in the surface sense-organs of sight, hearing, small, taste and touch.' And the conception or idea of a thing is *temporal*, '[our ideas of things], instead of appearing spread out simultaneously and horizontally in space, are made by the truth-sense to appear strung together successively and longitudinally; which is to say, in a chain of *causes and effects*, in a *time-chain*'.[56] It is the capacity for the latter variety of experience that is distinct to the human ego; and this is said to be entirely down to the Power of the Word. 'It is not held, as we hold, that language is the creator of Mind', claims Marsden.[57] 'Language put the individual man [...] into possession of an order of images hitherto inexperienced: the introspective image isolating and embodying a thing's meaning.'[58] In fact, Marsden can be said to have anticipated the 'linguistic turn' in philosophy initiated later in the century by the writings of Saussure and Heidegger, when she says human being is cognate with the power to create and manipulate signs. 'It created the *imaginary image*, and at a single stroke laid the foundations of the worlds of thought and imagination', insists Marsden. 'Instead of an organism which was merely conscious, it created an organism which was self-conscious.'[59]

Systematically re-creating from within myself (by processes of association and imitation) aspects of things apart from those things, I project a secondary world, a world within my world, in which space is eliminated, and patterns of cause and effect emerge, as each *complex* is reduced by the white heat of a human intellect, likened to 'laboratory conditions which will favour the rapid disintegration and simplification of ideas'.[60] As Marsden explains, 'search for truth, which resolves itself into a search for causal connexions between the various elements of our experience, has to run counter to the accidental associative inter-attractions established by the experience of them under the chance contiguities of a personal time and space'.[61] The *association of ideas*, far from being a mechanism for innovation, produces only the *vagueness* that constitutes the tyranny of Mind postulated by Stirner. In contrast, Marsden believes 'the labour of truth becomes largely the attempt to dissolve the accidental assemblies which have thus coagulated as units of appearance into elements related by a connexion more causal'.[62] This process of 'reduction' or 'definition' should, in Marsden's opinion, be the single purpose of every modern philosopher. 'But its action is *not* limited to the creation of this fine inner duplicate of the outer world', she writes. 'Its most striking activity is its power to double-back, by means of its word-created inner replicas, upon the things of the outer world, and by doing so inaugurate the kind of activity we call *causal* or *constructive*.'[63] In doing so an individual goes beyond the tyranny of the Word to become essentially 'The Maker'. 'By virtue of being the Creator of an inner spirit world he becomes the Artificer of a new and fabricated outer world', writes Marsden.[64] 'The concept once framed will turn into a reality, and through knowledge will control the whole vital mechanism of life.'[65] As in Stirner, the triumph of the idea culminates in a third phase of being beyond the current transitional human age, and in the overwriting of our species in the creation of a higher; 'a species which will "know" all things, because it will have completed the time nexus, the causal nexus, from start to finish, joined origins with ends, and made death and life plain. With power, too, to control them.'[66] In fact, Marsden reflects, 'The power to create and apply a sign which in him creates knowledge will therefore eventually vindicate that deep wisdom which is attributed to the serpent when he led Eve on to eat of the tree of knowledge so that she and her kind should not die but should become even as the gods – immortal.'[67] But here Marsden can be seen to break with Stirner – and on precisely the issue she had anticipated in 1912, on first reviewing *The Ego and Its Own*: that is to say, her superhuman ego *is* whatever absolute it can define and realize, and not nothing. 'Let therefore the genius arrive who can give limits and features to the Godhead, and it becomes a question of time before the God is duly "realized".'[68]

The Imagism of Ezra Pound

To fulfil the full potential of a human ego thus necessarily means being scientist or artist; capable of refining one's inward then reconfiguring the outward World, the difference between science and art is said to be not a difference of method, but of subject matter. 'If science is the knowledge gained by applying to non-vital phenomena, a method of accurate description as opposed to that of imaginative interpretation, art is the product of the same method applied to vital (and mainly humanly vital) phenomena.'[69] But while science has made tremendous advances over the past 300 years, 'because during this period it has trusted to the results of unprejudiced observation of the "thing"', art, on the other hand, remains 'in a position analogous to that in which science was, when astronomy was astrology, chemistry alchemy, and mathematics witchcraft, that is, when scientists looked at facts but with a preconceived idea, a thought, interpolated between facts and their intelligence of them'.[70] (That is to say, in the Shamanic phase of the Stirnerian history.) Art is in a state of stagnation because it has lost touch with what is vital in its subject. 'Its associations have all been with the concrete and the static, and life which reveals itself to the intellect only when it moves, in its moments of change, is an enigma.'[71] Now, following so many wasted centuries of creative energy, Marsden calls for artists to begin humbly with the 'thing'.[72] 'The human brain can work to fruitful purpose only when it is set to ply about images which sprung into vivid form in the human consciousness: it is at home only in that aura of images which is thrown off from the living "I" and to which men have given the title of "The World".'[73]

The reactivation of the latent energies of the poet/artist was a matter of pressing concern for Marsden: 'A great poet is, in fact, a great limiting agency who is able to develop the Finite out of the Infinite, and it is as such that popular respect goes out to him.'[74] Indeed, it is the poet/artist who combines the capacity for *imaging* philosophy possesses (in altogether too great a degree) with the *realizing* powers of science: 'The great artist would be the Mind which could achieve the synthesis of the two – imaging and realizing: such a Mind as would be able to apprehend the new vision so clearly that he could recreate and reproduce it with precision.'[75] To this end, Marsden was to open her journal, on the suggestion of her colleague Rebecca West, to a young poet newly arrived from the Mid-West of America and the rag-tag of writers he had momentarily marshalled into something resembling a movement. Now widely recognized as an opening salvo in the Modernist assault on the literary tradition, the Imagism of Ezra Pound has hitherto been regarded by historians of Imagism and by Marsden's biographers as a rude imposition. In the earliest account of the transaction we read that 'Forthwith an agreement was reached under the terms of which the literary group was to do as it liked with the whole paper, except for the leading article, which was always to be written by Miss Marsden.'[76] And according to Glenn Hughes, 'What she wrote had not the slightest connection with the other contents of the paper.'[77] This account has been thoroughly discredited by correspondence uncovered by pioneering research on the part of Bruce Clarke: but while he proves that Marsden retained her control over the management of her magazine, his emphasis on her editorial performance can only imply, not establish, that there must be some significant parallel between the poetry appearing there and the philosophy underpinning the magazine. 'Clarke references Stirner several times, but displays little interest in Stirner and how Marsden actually used *The Ego and Its Own*.'[78] And having reviewed the evidence in Clarke's book, John F. Welsh comes to the conclusion that there is nothing in the suggestion that Marden's egoism is in any way related to Imagist poetry. 'The former is concerned with the domination of thought and persons by fixed, abstract, collectivist constructs', he writes. 'The latter is a rejection of naturalism and realism in art and literature.'[79] As Marsden's most recent biographer (Lee Garner) points out, the editor herself professed to see little connection between the two halves of the journal – confiding to Harriet Shaw Weaver that it 'has no unity; it is not vitalised or dominated by any united purpose which can be made to grow increasingly attractive and intelligible to readers'. And Marsden blames the dull weight of Imagism, saying that 'It is not bright because it has no leaven: what should be the yeast to lighten the heaviness of Egoism is the equally unleavened heaviness of Imagism [...] a deadening combination.'[80]

But one must remember that Ezra Pound expressed similar reservations about the Imagists. There is a marked discrepancy between the theories of Pound and the practice of most Imagists: ... a discrepancy that would result in him leaving the group in order to promote a newer, more rigorous form of Imagism, called Vorticism. The two warring camps within the magazine, their mutual discontent, must not prevent an objective appraisal of the similarities that undoubtedly exist between Marsden's egoist philosophy and the 'doctrines' of Imagism as defined by Pound. As David Moody has observed, in the most recent book to touch upon this subject (the first volume in his new biography of Ezra Pound) there is in fact real affinity between the two – 'such that each could provide an illuminating commentary upon the other'.[81] The parallels are said to include an emphasis on the creative virtue of the egoist/artist, the interdictions placed on convention and abstraction, the idea that god is a state of mind, manifest when a state of mind takes form, and that a man becomes a god when he enters such a state of mind. 'As specific instances [Pound] might have mentioned "Δωρια" and "The Return", or "In a Station of the Metro" ...'[82] Indeed, one might be tempted to think these poems had been selected in order to reveal the affinities between Pound's Imagism and Marsden's concerns. But Moody goes on to reaffirm the view there is no meeting of these two like minds. 'Though [Marsden] printed Pound's "Contemporania"', Moody explains, 'she didn't read them; and nor did she read Joyce's *A Portrait of the Artist* when that was running as *The Egoist*'s serial for over a year and a half in 1914 and 1915.'[83] And though Moody is probably right to suggest that Pound took very little interest in the views of his editor in the three months he worked for the magazine, the available evidence will simply not support the view that Marsden was equally disinterested in Pound (and Joyce). The keen interest that Marsden took in both writers is evident in her correspondence with Pound and Harriet Shaw Weaver. In the summer of 1913, Marsden thoroughly interrogated Pound before offering him the pages he desired in her journal: 'I have been questioned earnestly and by a person certainly of good will', explains Pound, in his essay 'The Serious Artist' (1913). 'We are asked to define the relation of the arts to economics, we are asked what position the arts are to hold in the ideal republic.'[84] Her playful familiarity with Pound on the one hand, and her being prepared to go to prison for printing Joyce on the other must undermine the old misconception that Marsden held no interest in the young Modernists she had taken under her wing. The very 'real affinities' that can be shown to consist between these two theories set out in *The Egoist* (egoism and Imagism) must at last be recognized as something other than the 'comic' coincidence it is made out to be by Moody (in what, one should point out, is otherwise a very accurate and rigorous appraisal). If the extent to which the poet was aware of such congruities remains open to question, there is no longer any reason whatsoever for assuming Marsden's editorial intelligence to be anything other than entirely in control, backing Pound's literary experiment, in order to further her own specific agenda.

Marsden had declared a war on abstractions, on thought divorced from feeling; had called for the artists to begin as a scientist must with an unprejudiced observation of the 'thing' – the latter being the images thrown off from the living 'I'.[85] And on the most basic level the Imagist poets did reaffirm the need for a preliminary linguistic-hygiene (though many can hardly be said to have achieved this modest aim). 'Go in fear of abstractions', wrote Pound, 'no superfluous word, no adjective, which does not reveal something'.[86] In *Poetry*, March 1913, F.S. Flint had anticipated Marsden's rallying call for 'Direct treatment of the "thing"', and this injunction can be seen to underpin everything produced by Pound's friend William Carlos Williams, over the decades that would follow; in *Paterson* (1946) that poet would repeat, as though a mantra, the phrase, 'No ideas but in things!'[87] As to whether Marsden and the Imagists were referring to quite the same 'thing' is questionable at least. Flint's 'thing' can be either 'subjective or objective' and though it is clear to Moody that a 'thing' here is evidently a 'Thing-in-the-mind' (is already a subjective mental object), to insist (as he does) that Pound must have been thinking of such a 'thing' is to credit him with altogether too great a knowledge and interest in the phenomenological philosophies that preoccupied his editor. In her columns, Marsden herself took her Imagists in hand for failing to recognize precisely this point. 'Our friends, the "Imagists",' she writes, 'have taken exception, oddly enough, to the use of the adjective: because they hate generalization and abstractions. But…every form of the verb indeed save that which is hitched up to the first person singular is a danger to accuracy and expression.' She concludes with the observation that 'Accurately, every sentence begins with "I".'[88]

What one can say is that Marsden would have been predisposed to regard at least the very first Imagist poems she encountered as examples of the new art she had hailed in an article on 'Intellect and Culture' on 1 July 1913: an art which would be record of Soul moving consciously in Light; 'the living impulse in its complex totality: the sum-total of all the attractions of all its lives in one complex retort.'[89] For all the material relating to Imagism available at that point must have seemed to anticipate Marsden's own thinking on the matter. In *Poetry* March 1913, Pound had published 'A Few Don'ts By An Imagiste', a piece in which he uses a Lockean term, *complex*, in the technical sense employed by the new psychologists, such as Hart (the first translator of Freud); that is, as 'experienced emotion' rather than pure Idea. 'An "Image" is that which presents an intellectual and emotional complex in an instant of time', explains

Pound. 'It is the presentation of such a "complex" instantaneously which gives that sense of sudden liberation; that sense of freedom from time limits and space limits; that sense of sudden growth, which we experience in the presence of the greatest works of art.'[90] In American journal *Forum* a year earlier in 1912, Pound had even stated that 'What the analytical geometer does for space and form, the poet does for the states of consciousness', had called for poetry to be regarded as a 'formula' or an 'equation'.[91]

> 'By the signs $a^2 + b^2 = c^2$, I imply a circle', 'By $(a-r)^2 + (b-r)^2 = (c-r)^2$, I imply the circle and its mode of birth. I am led from the consideration of the particular circles formed by my ink-well and my table-rim, to the contemplation of the circle absolute, its law; the circle free in all space, unbounded, loosed from the accidents of time and place'.[92]

And had Marsden known nothing of these articles, the poems that Pound submitted to her journal must in themselves have seemed the most perfect vindication of her own hopes for the medium; a new mode of poetry that would represent that psychological process whereby the mind converts an object into Idea. 'In a poem of this sort', says Pound, 'one is trying to record the precise instant when a thing outward and objective transforms itself, or darts into a thing inward and subjective'.[93] To approach Pound's Imagist poetry through the theoretical framework developed by Marsden is to read them again with new light.

> The apparition of these faces in the crowd;
> Petals on a wet, black bough.

The movement of the poem must appear to emulate that sudden turn inward, from the object to subject: the 'apparition' of the phenomenal world is replicated in the very moment of its passing, burning an after-image in the mind's-eye, and bound in a dense of web of emotion and memory – an association of accidental ideas that the poet must cut through, the intellectual and emotional complex that he must refine, in order to render, realize, represent – and that not as description but *equation*. We cannot know quite when Pound first began to talk of reducing his poem from thirty lines to two over the course of a year and a half (he would first publish a written account of its creation in his book on Gaudier-Brzeska and Vorticism in 1916), but the poem itself is an implicit rebuke to the 'verbalising' Marsden detested. Her decision to follow publication of Pound's 'Contemporania' with a leading article from that same writer (in the place of Marsden's usual slot) on the subject of 'The Serious Artist' (an essay written at Marsden's instigation) must be taken as a measure of the extraordinary extent to which Marsden had begun to believe in the potential of this new psychological mode of poetry – and its young American inventor.

So too, the palpable disappointment in Marsden's published response to Pound, his unexpected reversion to a fuzzily defined late-Romanticism. 'There is, about artists when asked to define their business, a coyness which would be exquisitely ludicrous if it were evinced by chemists or mathematicians, by carpenters or brick-layers', she begins. 'This coyness, and the vague waving of hands to give the expression of helplessness, in-a-sort, in the grip of some high force, which, if not divine, is at least too much above the common level to be comprehended by the Philistine, or the common-sense man – these are quite sufficient to place art as we now know it, in its sub-conscious period.'[94] The fissure that would open up between the literary and philosophical content of the journal, as Imagism slipped further from Pound's control (and devolved into a sort of literary impressionism under the aegis of Amy Lowell), might perhaps be traced to this precise moment. However that might be, Pound's failure to theorize his Modernist practice did not mean an immediate end to the Imagist presence at *The Egoist* (far from it): and there is even evidence to suggest that the two components within the journal, Marsden's egoism and Pound's Imagism, began to impact upon each other from this point on.

Marsden's thought was at its best when sharpened by controversy, and much that is important in her philosophy as developed in 'Lingual Psychology' finds its first formulation in her critique of Pound, as she attempts to explain that art is not yet science because practitioners of the former, though they are to be commended for seeking to break with the 'Verbal' in order to reconnect with the 'Vital', still labour under the misapprehension that their poem must 'present' rather than refine a 'complex'. 'In poetry the swerve away from the stupidity of convention has likewise been caught up by free thought, by the fancy unattached to reality', she observes. 'A perfect example of a genuine emotional impulse being rendered abortive by plunging it into ideas is given by the work of F.T. Marinetti, the futurist leader, who expounds his creed in the current issue of "Poetry and Drama".'[95] Dismissing the contemporary literary vogue for the unexpurgated representation of Radical Empiricism's *stream of consciousness* or psychological flux (culmination of Schopenhauer's suggestion that 'sensation' might be our root in the 'real'), Marsden argues that poetry is or should be

'highest manifestation of self-consciousness, *re*-presented in terms
of self-recognised emotion.'[96] Indeed, having considered the special
possibilities of music, drama and art, poetry is held to be something
apart from the rest; as it is (or should be) in poetry alone that emotion
rounds on itself, articulate, and says, 'I know you.'[97] 'That is the broad
difference between prose and poetry (not rhyme and poetry) – a
difference which we, unlike Mr. Pound, think it worthwhile inquiring
into.'[98] Drawing upon the analogy earlier deployed by Pound in his
article for *Forum*, Marsden argues that poetry is a formula 'simply
because in poetry all the evidence of laboratory work is removed.'[99] In
fact, 'Poetry is the expression of the soul-motion: perfect knowledge
free both of redundance and hesitancy: is brief because it is reduced
to the exact equivalent: it has reached the completeness of knowledge
when its dimensions can be expressed in a formula.'[100] Marsden's
thinking on the poetry of egoism (which is far from being clear in
her earlier article 'Intellect and Culture') is building on the insights
and oversights of Imagism, and is beginning to acquire that unique
emphasis upon the egoistic reduction of the complex idea that would
prove so important to the later 'Lingual Psychology'.

Imagism itself was a lost cause. Consisting for the most part of
neo-Hellenist poets with little time or sympathy for Pound's 'Doctrine
of the Image' quite apart from the egoism of Marsden, the movement
soon lost what little coherence it had ever possessed, and would
swiftly fade into irrelevance, with the onset of the First World War.
But Marsden's waspish editorial can be seen to have stung Pound
into clarifying his terminology in his later writing on Imagism.
In the *Fortnightly Review* (1914), for instance, Pound inveighs against
the symbolists, who dealt in 'association' and contrasts their use of

symbols (that have fixed values like numbers in arithmetic), to the Imagists *images*, which 'have a variable significance like the signs a, b, and x in algebra'.[101] And in a retrospective for *The New Age*, published January 1915, Pound reproduces a further distinction first set out by Marsden when he adds that the moment some external scene or action is seized upon by emotion and carried to the mind must then be followed by a process whereby 'that vortex purges it of all save the essential or dominant or dramatic qualities, and it emerges like the external original'. The Image, Pound explains, is more than an idea: 'It is a vortex or cluster of fused ideas and is endowed with energy. If it does not fulfil these specifications, it is not what I mean by an Image.'[102] There is thus the tantalizing possibility that Marsden helped to provoke Pound's break with an ill-defined Imagism in order to participate in that altogether more rigorous movement known as Vorticism. 'You may think of man as that toward which perception moves', he declares in the Vorticist journal *BLAST* (1914). 'You may think of him as the TOY of circumstance, as plastic substance RECEIVING impressions.' And having repeated Marsden's line of attack on Marinetti's 'impressionism of speed', Pound sets out the alternative: 'OR you may think of him as DIRECTING a certain fluid force against circumstance, as CONCEIVING instead of merely observing and reflecting.'[103] In point of fact, Vorticism is known to have drawn heavily on egoist philosophy (being based in large part on an alternative reading of Stirner) and this circumstance serves to underline the extent to which Marsden's overlooked philosophical writing was, far from being peripheral, participating in a discourse that underpins much of what we now think of as being most vital in Modernist pre-war thought.

Certainly, Marsden's formulation of a theoretical basis for Modernist experiment merits far greater recognition than the one brief acknowledgement her grand project receives in the epic *Spring and All* by William Carlos Williams (1923). Noting that a terrific confusion has taken place, that emptiness stares us in the face, that no man knows where to turn, Williams asks a series of questions: Whither? and To what end? Has life its tail in its mouth or its mouth in its tail? Why are we here? At once enchanted and baffled and on his guard against Marsden's work – is the reference to her writing that follows merely another sign of the times, or is Williams seriously suggesting that these columns in *The Egoist* are where we should be looking for the answers? In any case, there it is: 'Dora Marsden's Philosophic Algebra.'[104]

Philosophic Algebra

In addition to promoting Imagist poetry, Marsden's journal famously published three seminal pieces of Modernist fiction as serials: *A Portrait of the Artist as a Young Man* and *Ulysses* by James Joyce and *Tarr* by the Vorticist writer and artist Wyndham Lewis. Both writers can be seen to engage heavily with Stirnerian egoism prior to the First World War, and in these three books in particular the reader will find perhaps the most compelling psychological treatments of the Stirnerian subject. It is in the fiction rather than the poetry published by *The Egoist* that Marsden's faith in Modernism found its great vindication. But perhaps the most interesting reflections relating to Stirner on the part of these writers occur in work produced in the twenties, after the journal had ceased publication, as each writer adapted the philosophy in radically different ways. I will therefore consider this writing in the next essay. Before doing so, I would like to close by considering the great problem inherent to Marsden's interpretation of Stirnerian egoism: a problem that both Lewis and Joyce would later struggle with – and I should like to end where I began: with the re-evaluation of T.S. Eliot's position on Stirnerian egoism in his poetical and theoretical writing. Completed just months before he joined *The Egoist* in 1917, Eliot's long unpublished doctoral thesis *Knowledge and Experience in the Philosophy of F.H. Bradley* offers an incisive and devastating critique of the psychological and epistemological theories prevalent before the First World War, that is readily applied, with relatively little difficulty, to Marsden's own 'Lingual Psychology'.

It will be remembered that Marsden at times seems to echo the *Appearance and Reality* of F.H. Bradley, but her philosophy can be seen to repeat precisely the mistake that both Bradley and Eliot warn against: that is to say, Marsden regards the sensations of the world as mere adjectives of the 'I'. According to Bradley and Eliot, we have the right to say that the world is a construction but not that it is *my* construction: 'for in that way "I" am as much "my" construction as the world is'.[105] Instead, Bradley and Eliot insist the phenomenal world is a construction out of 'finite centres', and that these 'points of view' are *not* to be considered identical with individual human consciousness (or 'soul'). In fact, we may be said to move from one 'finite centre' to another when we become aware there are alternative points of view, and then determine an object by another relation (that is to say, when

I change my mind).[106] 'There could be no such thing, we may say, as a single finite centre, for every experience implies the existence of something independent of the experience, something capable, therefore, of being experienced differently, and the recognition of this fact is already the transition to another point of view', explains Eliot.[107] 'It is this transition from one point of view to another which is known to Mr Bradley's readers as transcendence.'[108]

For Bradley, our transcending the finite experience that comprises our self and our world is possible because all is present in the Absolute. For Eliot, on the other hand, Bradley's universe, actual only in finite centres, is only by an act of faith unified, and upon inspection must fall away into the isolated finite experiences out of which it is put together: 'Pretending to be something which makes finite centres cohere, [the Absolute] turns out to be merely the assertion that they do.'[109] Every movement from one point of view to another takes place in the void, is underwritten by nothing but faith: 'every transformation of type involves a leap which science cannot take, and which metaphysics must take', he concludes. 'It involves an interpretation, a transmigration from one world to another, and such a pilgrimage involves an act of faith.'[110] As Eliot would write many years later in his Four Quartets (1935–1942), 'the pattern is new in every moment/And every moment a new and shocking/ Valuation of all we have been'; though 'not escaping from the past/ Into different lives, or into any future', we must remain true to our calling as 'Travellers' and 'Fare forward'.[111] To do otherwise, to resist this voyage into the dark, is to commit oneself to a finite experience, rather than meeting alternative points of view that must bring on the necessary evacuation, that *ekstasis*, that moment of ecstasy, that compels me to go beyond everything that I am. 'The point of view (or finite centre) has for its object one consistent world, and accordingly no finite centre can be self-sufficient, for the life of a soul does not consist in the contemplation of one consistent world but in the painful task of unifying (to a greater or less extent) jarring and incompatible ones, and passing, when possible, from two or more discordant view points to a higher which shall somehow include and transmute them.'[112]

In contrast, Marsden presents us with a prospect of endless elaboration without transcendence: rather than dying from moment to moment, Marsden's personal point of view – encompassing the polarities of self and the world – is expected to survive even physical death. 'Unlike the parent force out of which they spring, these differentiating influences [i.e. body and world] are successive, transient, impermanent', writes Marsden, in her penultimate column for *The Egoist* 'How the Theory of the Ego Requires Us to Construe Death'. 'While the body dissolves, and with it the world, the power of consciousness survives as a potentiality... [an] indestructible unit.'[113] In Marsden's philosophy, the ego as sum of individual consciousness is conceived to be 'the underlying permanent stuff of our universe'. And so what Eliot terms the 'life of the soul' *is* the contemplation (reduction, definition, analysis) of that 'one consistent world' which each personality might (through the sign-making power of the intellect and resulting mastery of space and time) eventually overwrite – and thereby become. As previously noted, Marsden's superhuman ego *is* whatever absolute it can define and realize. And there is a contradiction here that must be seen to undermine Marsden's entire system.

For the egoist performing a supposedly comprehensive analysis must remain impervious to self-analysis: ruling that the 'nothing' that is key to the theory and practice of Stirnerian egoism is a 'bogus conception', Marsden insists ego cannot negate everything that it is. 'The idea of negation is a valid and extremely useful one, but its absolute employ is made impossible by the possible basis of feeling', she writes.[114] 'The idea of negation is in fact nothing greater than an instrument of differentiation between one positive state of feeling and another ... to abstract some given feature from any given complex of feeling.' This complex may indeed be widened in extent until it is coterminus with the whole universe of feeling, the negative idea abstracting everything from the whole: everything, that is, save the *power to feel*. 'It can only be applied within the limits of that positive base', concludes Marsden. 'It modifies the features of such positive states but it cannot negate the entire state.'[115] In Bradleyan terms, the ego is committed to a personal point of view, a finite centre of experience; and though a personality might well become the god of that universe, no shock of encounter with any *other* can bring the great and terrible change which compels us to become strangers to ourselves for a moment, a moving spirit. 'The natural wakeful life of our Ego is a perceiving', muses the protagonist of Eliot's poem 'Coriolan', recalling Edmund Husserl and the question that follows from that; 'How then can *Consciousness itself* separate out as a *concrete thing in itself*, from that within it, of which we are conscious, namely, the *perceived being, "standing over against"* consciousness *"in and for itself"*?'[116]

Having laboured so hard to be free of 'fixating forces', to maintain herself in 'pure onward motion', Marsden's interpretation of egoist theory ultimately precluded flight from her own self-conception: and she would lose herself in her work as a direct result.[117] Marsden had once made a distinction between *thought* and *thinking*, stating that the latter is a process that liberates living impulses ready for action rather than binding them up to construct a system: and yet this is precisely what Marsden would spend the rest of her life striving to achieve – retreating to a lonely cottage in the Lake District (with the name *Seldom Seen*) in order to work out *The Definition of the Godhead*, which she had promised in her final editorial for *The Egoist* in December 1919. Removing herself from a situation that afforded her an opportunity to gauge readerly response (and to receive critical feedback) Marsden produced two gargantuan volumes of theology (and these just the first in an unrealized series of seven) that profess to be nothing less than the answer to life, the universe and everything in it. 'It is common knowledge that philosophy, from the time of the Greeks (but, more especially, from the Cartesian age), has been held up by a problem having to do with the very nature of knowledge itself', she writes. 'To this has been given the name of the ego-centric predicament, and it consists in some supposed epistemological *reductio ad absurdum* in a problem known as that of solipsism.' According to Marsden, men of the present age can expect the solution in the form of that unique experiment that is due to appear at the summit of the evolutionary process. 'No man (in this present world-aeon) is as yet the One-in-the-Middle: the Great King: the Great Head who is definable as the One Ego having his centre in the world-centre and his boundaries in the boundaries of the entire world.'[118]

In *The New Freewomen* Marsden had once written that 'unless philosophers (pretentious title) are prepared to be proved in the wrong as well as in the right, to test their "guesses" in the open, vital truth will never progress beyond the closed systems of the individual cult-makers'.[119] In the decades of self-imposed isolation following the close of *The Egoist*, Marsden was to prove herself correct. In fact, there is a tantalizing parallel to the grand project undertaken by Joyce in similar conditions of *silence, exile and cunning*: the creation of a secondary, artificial reality that is based upon a comprehensive analysis of those systems through which we perceive and produce our world. But while the author of *Ulysses* and *Finnegans Wake* secured his 'cult', Marsden's Philosophic Algebra remains forgotten; a Bible that not, as yet, found its sect.

3

THE SIBERIA OF THE MIND

Wyndham Lewis

The Modernist as Egoist

A room in a great northern city; a typical student squat – pipes half-smoked, bed never-made, books piled on chair and table. Two are in Finnish. The third, 'stalely open', Arghol takes up to shut. It is the *Einige und Sein Eigenkeit* [*sic*]. 'One of the seven arrows' in this 'martyr's mind' – only this book, by renegade Hegelian Max Stirner, is named by Wyndham Lewis, and rejected. 'Poof! he flung it out of the window.'[1]

The gesture is timely. According to Paul Edwards, in his account of the artist, 'Stirner probably had little lasting influence upon Lewis.'[2] Unlike other sources Edwards cites as being central to an understanding of this radical 'play' entitled 'Enemy of the Stars', which appeared in the Vorticist journal *BLAST* in 1914, Stirner is not referred to again, does not survive the particularly rough handling he receives in this play. His book is condemned by Arghol as a 'parasite', with all the other books in the room, 'Poodles of the mind, Chows and King Charles', and is therefore torn up with the rest – left in 'a pile by the door ready to sweep out'.[3]

But in addition to marking the author's own break with Stirner, the incident curiously anticipates the general movement away from the philosophy of egoism that would take place during the war. Having enjoyed a period of intense interest in the English-speaking world following the publication of Byington's translation in 1912, *The Ego and His Own* was to vanish just as suddenly into obscurity again, as writers such as Joyce, Lewis and Marsden began to confront problems posed by new materialist theories of the mind (originating in Schopenhauer, developed over the course of the nineteenth-century by James and Bergson, and finding their culmination in the Behaviourist theory of the twentieth century). The world imagined in the play is already permeated with a strong sense of the extent to which mind is riddled with the unconscious, an 'underworld of energy and rebellious muscle', inextricably involved in the mechanism of a material universe in which stars are 'machines of prey'.[4]

However, Stirner is not rejected for his inadequacy, in the face of this radical new empiricist paradigm, but for precisely the reasons underpinning the action of renunciation in Stirner's own philosophy. 'Arghol's egoism is not the same as Stirner's', remarks Edwards, 'but his acts of repudiation of whatever fixes his ego in a false and unalterable shape are paralleled by Stirner's strategy of preventing any "ideal" or "property" from determining his ego'.[5] The joke is that in attempting to effect a catharsis, to purify ego of a philosophy which has been recognized as parasitic, Lewis's puppet is reiterating the very conditions that render such a renunciation necessary – and this is reflected in the way that Stirner's book *comes back* – to be rejected over and over again. A few minutes after hurling the book out into the street there is a knock at the door: the book is being returned by a shifting figure that assumes the guise of personalities that Arghol has tried to reject; the last being Stirner, as he imagines him: 'A middle aged man, red cropped head and dark eyes, self=possessed, loose, free, student-sailor, fingering the book.'[6] A comedy of inept renunciation follows. Stirner is bribed to 'go', but believes he is being offered the money for the book. This provokes a stinging rejoinder from the Hegelian. He flings the book at his disciple's head – 'its cover slaps him sharply' – and a scuffle ensues, resulting in Stirner's eviction.[7]

The book's capacity for returning unexpectedly is just as resonant as the fact of its rejection; – for the reception history of *The Ego and His Own* has been a sort of haunting. Having returned, in the pre-war era, from an obscurity so complete that Marx and Engels, Stirner's contemporaries, did not even bother to publish the refutation they had produced (*The German Ideology*), the book has persisted ever since, a ghost-like presence, only acknowledged in the moment of refutation or disavowal. And I would like to suggest that the deeply inadequate exorcism performed by Arghol in *The Enemy of the Stars* in 1914, could serve as a symbol for Lewis's own relationship with this early influence in the four monumental books that author produced in the inter-war era: *The Art of Being Ruled* (1926), *Time and Western Man* (1927), *Childermass* (1928) and *The Apes of God* (1930). Long after Stirner is thought to have ceased to matter in Lewis's writing, visual imagery that, in the pre-war material, is quite clearly derived from *The Ego and His Own*, can be seen to persist, in relation to a recurring pattern of associated ideas. Edwards has speculated that Lewis's later interest in anthropology might be rooted in Stirner: 'It is possible', says Edwards, 'that Stirner's characterisation of philosophical idealism as a variety of "Mongolian" shamanism led Lewis to ethnological accounts such as Mary Czaplicka's, on Siberia (which he quotes in *The Art of Being Ruled*).'[8] In fact, the development of this trope – that of Siberian shamanism – in the later theoretical writing has been very helpful in facilitating the interpretation of much that had been left obscure in *The Enemy of the Stars*, particularly those passages relating to gender. The following essay suggests that the specifically Stirnerian take on shamanism in the pre-war work is likewise a potential aid to understanding the writing of the 1920s, that Stirner might well provide the 'key' that many commentators have felt to be 'missing' from *The Art of Being Ruled* and the rest. In the course of tracing what remains of the egoist paradigm in Lewis's great period, this essay establishes that Stirner persisted, a revenant, to trouble the literature of Modernism more generally in the inter-war era.

A portrait of the artist as a young Shaman

Begin with this summary: what is known concerning the shamanism of Siberia in *The Enemy of the Stars*. The play is set in a wheelwright's yard, 200 miles south of the Arctic circle.[9] Here Arghol has come to work for his uncle, and is kicked to within an inch of his life by this 'super' once every 24 hour. Since arriving he has acquired a disciple called Hanp, who despises his hero for his weakness and envies him for his former social life in Berlin. The characters are of a physical type taken 'from broad faces where Europe grows arctic, intense, human and universal'.[10] Such references to the Asian steppes occur throughout. At one point, in what must be quite literally the most far-fetched metaphor in the play, Arghol and Hanp are even compared to a dancing-girl and her Mongolian overlord.

> Harsh bayadere=shepherdess of Pamir, with her Chinese beauty: living on from month to month in utmost tent with wastrel, lean as mandrake root, red and precocious: with heavy black odour of vast Manchurian garden-deserts, and the disreputable muddy gold squandered by the unknown sun of the Amur.[11]

Marked for 'fate of sovereign prostitution', Arghol is the 'bayadere=shepherdess of Pamir;' repeatedly likened to a woman, the character is said to project a 'TYPE OF FEMININE BEAUTY CALLED "MANISH"'.[12] The reasoning underlying these passages becomes clearer when one considers the text in relation to Lewis's later writing on shamanic magic in *The Art of Being Ruled*, where he explains that "Throughout the entire history of the subject, homosexuality and male transformation of sex have been more or less associated in men's minds with magic and witchcraft."[13] Over the course of two chapters Lewis argues that the *Shaman* is the logical result of a common belief among primitive peoples in the superior magical power women possess over men. In such circumstances, says Lewis, it is natural men should have come to think that one of the first steps towards a career as a magician was to change their sex. 'It is the example of a far-sighted calculation or strategy: one of the maddest flights of primitive human cunning attempting to harness supernatural energy by a *feigning*, for the easily deceived powers of the natural world, of femininity.'[14]

For the Vorticist such an 'escape by artifice from the iron rules of physical laws', must necessarily merit some measure of praise.[15] The achievement is, at the very least, on a par with that of the hairdresser blessed in Lewis's journal: 'He attacks Mother Nature for a small fee … correcting the grotesque anachronisms of our physique.'[16] In *The Caliph's Design* (1919), a manifesto for a new architecture published shortly after the First World War, Lewis remarked upon the creative capabilities of certain beetles, their capacity for turning form and colour impulses into living flesh:

> These beetles can convert their faces into hideously carved and detestable masks, can grow out of their bodies menacing spikes, and throw up on top of their heads sinister headdresses, overnight. Such changes in their personal appearance, conceived to work on the psychology of their adversaries, is possibly not a very profound or useful invention, but it is surely a considerable feat. Any art worth the name is, at the least, a feat of this description. The New Guinea barred and whitewashed masks are an obvious parallel. As to the wing mechanism that first lifted a creature off the ground, and set it spinning or floating through the air, you must call Shakespeare in to compete with it.[17]

The Shaman's achievement is of the same order. 'The actual appearance of a transformed *shaman* is not that of the "mongolian" imbecile of our clinics, but is a mask of fixed wild pathos', writes Lewis: 'Borgoraz describes it exactly when he says it is a female mask of tragedy.'[18]

Like the Oceanic masks that Picasso and Epstein imitated in their art, the transformative magic practised by the Shaman upon his own body is hailed by Lewis as a prototype of modern art. In *Time and Western Man* (1927), Lewis states that 'creative art is a spell, a talisman, an incantation – that it is magic, in short', and notes that 'The poet or philosopher in the non-religious greek states occupied, we are told, much the same position as the priest or witch-doctor or magician in a more religious or superstitious community.'[19] He concludes that 'For me art is the civilised *substitute* for magic; as philosophy is what, on a higher or more complex plane, takes the place of religion.'[20]

Note though: this distinction is not perfectly clear in *The Caliph's Design* and *The Art of Being Ruled*. Lewis repeatedly attempts to conflate the 'Arctic Hysteria' of the Shaman with what he considered throughout his life to be the very highest form of literary art: the nineteenth-century Russian novel. 'The epileptic naïf and mystical element', speculates Lewis in *The Art of Being Ruled*, 'in nearly all nineteenth-century russian literature has no doubt some relation to this extreme inconstancy and collapsibility of the Siberian peoples.'[21] In *BLAST 1*, Lewis even goes so far as to suggest that his reason for 'very genuine optimism' regarding the potential of radical art in England, consists primarily in the extent to which the latter resembles Siberia: 'England is just as unkind and inimical to Art as the Arctic zone is to Life', Lewis explains. 'As the steppes and the rigours of the Russian winter, when the peasant has to lie for weeks in his hut, produces that extraordinary acuity of feeling and intelligence we associate with the Slav; so England is just now the most favourable country for the appearance of a great art.'[22] In being described in terms that suggest he is a form of Shaman, is subject to this 'Arctic hysteria', Arghol might then be taken to be a symbol of the modern artist in that 'Siberia of the mind' that is England.[23]

In what is the seminal reading of this extraordinarily difficult piece of writing, Edwards suggests that the Siberian imagery in Lewis derives from the schematic history provided by Stirner in *The Ego and His Own* – in which he identifies three phases. According to Stirner, we escape from our 'Negroid' state of subservience to the material fact by entering a second, rather more subtle state of submission to things of the spirit or mind; these being gods and spirits at first, then concepts such as the 'State', 'love' and 'Humanity', for the sake of which people continue to practise self-renunciation. 'The shaman and the speculative philosopher mark the bottom and top rounds', according to Stirner, 'on the ladder of the *inward* man, the Mongol.'[24] The third phase is the 'Caucasian', and is to come about now that people begin to perceive that their own unique ego is the one absolute. Thus Arghol, 'a gladiator who has come to fight a ghost, Humanity', is a shaman or philosopher, in so far as he remains one of those who 'fight with ghosts, demons, *spirits*, gods'.[25] But this 'one in immense collapse' is equally the final result of Stirner's 'chronic philosophy'.[26] In Edwards's memorable phase, 'Arghol is the last shaman, struggling to realise the last remnant of the transcendental world of spirits, the Ego itself.'[27]

A note on 'The New Egos', published with 'The Enemy of the Stars' in *BLAST 1*, provides us with insights into how Lewis himself interpreted Stirner's historical schema. 'A civilised savage, in a desert=city', he begins, 'surrounded by very simple objects and restricted number of beings, reduces his Great Art down to the simple black human bullet'. He characterizes such sculpture as 'African' and states we have nothing to do with such sculpture. 'The African we have referred to cannot allow his personality to venture forth or amplify itself, for it would dissolve in vagueness of space', he writes. 'It has to be swaddled in a bullet=like lump.' In contrast, the 'modern town=dweller of our civilisation sees everywhere fraternal moulds for his spirit, and interstices of a human world'. We supplant the natural with a second man-made reality; and though life is really no more secure, his egotism less acute, society is sufficiently organized for him to permit 'his ego to walk abroad', until something akin to the self-effacement the egoist philosopher denounced – that which Lewis terms *impersonality* – becomes a sort of disease. 'Promiscuity is normal; such separating things as love, hatred, friendship are superseded by a more realistic and logical passion', Lewis claims. 'We all to=day (possibly with a coldness reminiscent of the insect=world) are in each other's vitals – overlap, intersect, and are Siamese to any extent.' According to Lewis, the result is that the old variety of egotism is 'no longer fit for such conditions as now prevail'; though the 'human form' continues to run like a wave through the 'texture or body of existence, and therefore of art', the isolated human figure of most ancient art (the 'African'?) is 'an anachronism' that should now be superseded. The character of these 'New Egos', and the new art that must result, is not spelt out. But Lewis seems to provide further details on this third phase in *The Ideal Giant*, a play that appeared in *The Little Review* in 1917, when his spokesman John Porter Kemp states the New Egos belong to either the Crowd or to the Artist. Each is an Ideal Giant – at once singular and many – representing two different ways of reconciling naïve egotism and impersonal truth.[28]

In Edwards's reading Arghol emerges as a problematic figure. On the one hand, he is making the right noises, echoing Stirner's complaint that every ego is from birth a criminal to begin with against the people, the State or Mankind in general, in saying that:

Self, sacred act of violence, is like murder on my face and hands. The stain won't come out. It is the one piece of property all communities have agreed it is illegal to posses. The sweetest=tempered person, once he discovers you are that sort of criminal, changes any opinion of you, and is on his guard.[29]

But the plan of action pursued by Arghol seems calculated to baffle and infuriate the philosopher he rejected. Having observed he loses something of his authentic Self in the course of everyday social interaction, Arghol has resolved to shrink in 'frosty climates' the 'immense snuffling or taciturn parasite' that battens upon him: the 'loathsome deformity' of a second or social Self.[30] Like Stirner, Arghol perceives that to 'walk abroad' is to risk an 'affliction got through indiscriminate rubbing against [his fellows]', the 'Famous men are those who have exchanged themselves against a thousand idiots' until the 'bastard form' infects the 'original solitude of the soul'.[31] But the steps he takes in order to preserve his ego from the impersonality of the modern town-dweller's insect-world mark a significant break with the path towards the realization of the Ideal Giant. Arghol has resolved to 'Accumulate in myself, day after day, dense concentration of pig-life'. With 'Nothing spent, stored rather in strong stagnation', he hopes to be 'rid at last of evaporation and lightness characteristic of men', and 'So burst Death's membrane through, slog beyond, not float in appalling distances'.[32]

In short, Arghol pursues a rearguard rather than a vanguard action – pushing back towards the phase of the civilized savage who 'cannot allow his personality to venture forth or amplify itself, for it would dissolve in vagueness of space' – has resolved to swaddle 'himself in a bullet=like lump'.[33]

In Edwards's persuasive explanation of 'The Enemy of the Stars' (developed further by Andrej Gasiorek), the first and secondary phases in Stirner's historical template are conflated with the dualistic opposition of matter and spirit set out in Schopenhauer's *The World as Will and Idea* – and which is ultimately derived from sources either Hindu or Gnostic. Arghol is 'something distant, terrible and eccentric' – i.e. the spirit or the divine spark that must be 'struck and banished from matter'.[34] But this Sophia is – perversely, Schopenhauer would say – trying to maintain her hold on the enemy territory of the stars or *archons*: the material universe. Arghol can only hope to maintain his precious individuality by holding the middle-ground between two mighty opposites: the ghosts of Future Mankind being at one with the red walls of the universe that close in upon this condemned protagonist.[35] The significance of this defeat is open to question. Edwards notes that the text will not permit us to affirm 'either that Arghol is a critique of Stirner's egoism [...] or that Arghol is revealed as a deluded character by Stirner's denunciation of his spiritual and ascetic ideals'.[36] But the inevitably of this failure is never in question. BLAST is a 'magazine programmatically contradictory and hence dualist'.[37] The outcome of the play is precisely 'what one would expect from an artist like Lewis who was sceptical about fantasies of the transcendence of dualism'.[38] In his hugely influential appraisal of the play, Edwards notes that Vorticism 'was not a movement that sought to transcend dualities, but to exploit them'.[39]

In relation to the play this interpretation may be regarded as perfectly correct. The universe Arghol inhabits is truly the creation of a demiurge – a minor and malicious god – that is to say, Lewis himself. In a sketch to accompany the text, Lewis depicts Arghol as a sculpture of the sort his friend Henri Gaudier-Brzeska might have created, a cross between a totem and a Swiss-army knife. In the text too, Arghol is described in terms that recall Epstein's Venus-figures: a 'barren muscular girl idol'. His head is that of a 'black, eagerly carved, herculean Venus', the fetish of an 'iron tribe, hyper barbarous'. 'Head heavy and bird=like, weighted to strike.'[40] Arghol is a puppet that cannot progress beyond the booth or arena that defines the action, but must remain inescapably caught between mind and matter, that is to say, between the printed page and the reader, the 'me' and 'you' in the preface said to perform this play 'very well'. If Arghol is unable to project the 'Ideal Giant' that seems to correspond to those 'New Egos' in the third phase of the Stirnerian teleology, this may explain why. Arghol is a portrait of the artist (as a young shaman); is a symbol merely – of that symbol for the modern artist; he is an *objet d'art*.

Indeed, it is tempting to consider Arghol in relation to Lewis's essay on puppet theatre in his collection of short stories *The Wild Body* (1927). In this piece Lewis introduces the puppets that appear in the stories as carefully selected specimens of religious fanaticism, worshippers of some fetish (a set of objects or one object in particular) that requires an unvarying ritual behaviour. 'Boswell's Johnson, Mr. Vennering, Malvolio, Bouvard and Pecuchet, the "commissaire" in Crime and Punishment, do not live', Lewis explains: 'they are congealed and frozen into logic, and an exuberant hysterical truth'.[41] Lewis then describes these puppets in terms that evoke the Siberian imagery developed in 'The Enemy of the Stars'. 'The chemistry of personality', he writes, '(subterranean in a sort of cemetery, whose decompositions are our lives) puffs up in frigid balls, soapy Snowmen, arctic carnival-masks, which we can photograph and fix.'[42] But if this confirms that Arghol is trapped in a Manichaean universe he cannot hope to transcend, Lewis also seems to be suggesting here that these decompositions are *our lives*. No less than Arghol, Lewis considers us all to be snowmen rather than shaman, however arctic our carnival-masks.

> First, to assume the dichotomy of mind and body is necessary here, without arguing it; for it is upon that essential separation that the theory of laughter here proposed is based. The essential us, that is the laugher, is as distinct from the Wild Body as in the Upanisadic account of the souls returned from the paradise of the Moon, which, entering into plants, are yet distinct from them. Or to take the symbolic vedic figure of the two birds, the one watching and passive, the other enjoying its activity, we similarly have to postulate two creatures, one that never enters into life, but that travels about in a vessel to whose destiny it is momentarily attached. That is, of course, the laughing observer, and the other is the Wild Body.[43]

The abdication of God

In this essay I want to break with the prevailing interpretation to argue that there persists between these polarities something more significant than the 'dead perfection' of a puppet's 'egotism', some other possibility beyond that recursion to a fetish-object.[44] For in that same book, *The Wild Body*, Lewis also celebrates the 'universal ego of the poet'; he is clearly not relinquishing his faith in a specifically Stirnerian synthesis when he praises that 'one synthetic and various ego'.[45] It is worth recalling here the distinction between person and individual the Bailiff insists upon in *The Childermass*. The personality of which Arghol and Lewis speak in 'The Enemy of the Stars' and 'Inferior Religions' is: 'that crusted fruity complex-and-finite reality – term by which we are accustomed to express the sensations of our empirical life – emerging in the matrix of Space and Time or Space-Time'.[46] The personality might be said to present a realist perspective on the Subject – and individuality, the idealist. 'Individuality then is identity without the idea of substance', the Bailiff explains (before observing this is out of fashion in the post-war era: 'It is not the persistent life of a bare universal that any man, ever, is likely to cover').[47] And as R.D. Laing observed, in *The Divided Self* (1959), there is no question here or anywhere of body-mind dualism, only two different ways of regarding the one thing, 'each the outcome of one's initial intentional act'.[48] That one universal and synthetic ego of which Lewis speaks in *The Wild Body* can therefore be neither personality nor individuality thus defined. When Arghol opposes personality to mankind in the following passage, it is not the Stirnerian ego to which he refers, but to that ego as posited. Not that nothing that permits me to stand apart, that separates myself from what I am, but that which I am, that being I represent me to myself as being – my cause, my sake, my persona.

Between Personality and Mankind it is always a question of dog & cat; they are diametrically opposed species. Self is the ancient race, the rest are the new one. Self is the race that lost. But Mankind still suspects Egotistic plots, and hunts Pretenders.[49]

No doubt everyone is, potentially, a Quixote/Falstaff/Pecksniff/ Arghol. Such comic types are part of our own organism: an imitation and standardizing of self that implies the existence of a human norm.[50] Nonetheless every living being possesses (in varying degrees) the power to be a creator, a minor god. In a series of 'Imaginary Letters', published in *The Little Review* (May 1917–April 1918), Lewis expresses, through his surrogate William Bland Burn, his belief that a writer such as Shakespeare or Cervantes is a 'Colossus' capable of projecting the sort of 'play-world' that those who have chosen to settle for being mere puppets can only hope to inhabit. 'Wherever they go, there is a great crowd with them. Their brain is the record of their sympathies, people pour in and are piled up, with a persistent classification, until giant-like and permanent images, the "types" of drama or fiction are produced.'[51] The New Egos are not transcendental, but they *are* ecstatic – possessing a capacity for standing forth from the polarities (or rather perspectives) of body and soul – of personality and impersonality – in order to project a world.

Lewis develops these ideas further, in his book *Time and Western Man* (1927). In a chapter on 'God as Reality', Lewis insists that, as 'surface-creatures', we must reject those philosophies that predict or seek to effect transcendental union in the Absolute Synthesis. 'For such departures result in self-destruction, just as though we hurled ourself into space – into "mental-space", if you like, in this case.'[52] If Lewis believes in an Absolute (or God), he nevertheless believes that it is probably better, perhaps even more truthful, to pretend otherwise. 'This must be so for things to be bearable at all for us as creatures: for such unrelieved intimacy as would otherwise exist, such perpetual society – of such a pervasive, psychic, overwhelming kind – would not be socially possible.'[53] If there is a God, the very act of creation, in Lewis's system, necessarily required His abdication. 'He apparently no longer wished to be "the Absolute".'[54] This is no deprivation but a 'princely gift' that permits every one of us to realize our own *absolute* uniqueness:

> Human individuality is best regarded as a kind of artificial godhood. When most intensely separated from our neighbours and from all other things – most "ourselves", as we say – we are farthest away, clearly, from an Absolute, or any kind of Unity. Yet, in another sense, we are nearest to it.[55]

It is thus still possible to believe in a first-hand experience of the divine in human life. Dismissing those 'vulgar delusions' that privilege quantity, duration and scale, Lewis presents a radical take on Stirner's philosophy of 'creative negation', suggesting that we come closest to that nothingness-that-is-God-for-us in the act of creation: 'no Absolute need be ashamed of the feelings or thoughts of what we call a great artist or a great poet'.[56]

> To be at once perfectly concrete, we can assert that a God that swam in such an atmosphere as is produced by the music of a Bach fugue, or the stormy grandeur of the genii in the Sistine Ceiling, or the scene of the Judgement of Signorelli at Orvieto, who moved with the grace of Mozart – anyone may for himself

accumulate such comparisons from the greatest forms of art –
such a God would be the highest we could imagine ... [57]

The history of Pierpoint in *The Apes of God* (1930) provides
us with an insight into how this distinctively Lewisian twist on
Stirner's theories might play out. Pierpoint has removed himself
from London's 'artistic' circles prior to the start of the narration; has
since been successful in maintaining that absolute isolation Lewis
considers to be a prerequisite to artistic success. His relation to the
novel is therefore something like that of the artist in relation to his
work; the degraded society he reviews might be said to constitute
his own composition. So Pierpoint settles any lingering doubts we
might entertain concerning the situation that Arghol struggles with
in 'Enemy of the Stars'. In a letter circulated by Pierpoint (referred
to as an 'encyclical'), the artist begins by insisting upon, rather than
seeking to slur over, the fact that he too is a party; Pierpoint is (no
less than ourselves or Arghol) part of the universe he is attempting to
withdraw from, but this presents the true artist with no impediment
to his apotheosis.

> [It] is from amongst the parties that the acting judge is ultimately
> chosen. Where else should you get him from? The supreme
> judge is constantly absent. What we call a judge is a successful
> partisan. It is on account of the superior percentage of truth in the
> composition of your glosses that your statement is erected into
> a standard. And 'Of an opinion which is no longer doubted, the
> evidence ceases to be examined.' The finding of the supreme judge
> would automatically dissolve us all into limbo.[58]

But having refined himself out of existence this god is not content to remain behind or within or above his handiwork, to be as the Joycean artist, indifferent, paring his fingernails. 'I am not in agreement with the current belief in a strained "impersonality" as the secret of artistic success', states Pierpoint. An opinion that Lewis himself expressed in his critical appraisal of T.S. Eliot in *Men Without Art* (1934). In line with the approach advocated in that work, Pierpoint intervenes repeatedly, 'broadcasting' his opinions indirectly – via the medium of a puppet, that is to say, his voice carries clearest through everything that the artist is not. 'The flourishing and bombastic role that you may sometimes see me in, that is an effect of chance', Pierpoint explains. 'Or it is a caricature of some constant figure in the audience, rather than what I am (in any sense) myself. Or, to make myself clearer, it is my opposite.'[59] To underline the point, Pierpoint begins to broadcast through rival personas towards the end of the book. The two could not present a greater contrast. Starr-Smith is a Fascist Welshman: a tightly wound chauvinism that threatens imminent explosion, this figure suggests the 'simple black human bullet' of the 'civilised savage' in *BLAST 1*. Horace Zagreus, on the other hand, is a former actor and a part-time magician, acutely aware of his own emptiness and happy to play his part as a conduit for unknown powers: his 'polar-pelt' and transformational magic recall the early writing on the Shaman's 'arctic carnival mask'. Having apparently managed to evade fixation as either a fetish-object or a trepanned skull, the living ego is interjecting both false alternatives back into the narrative and is thereby reproducing the conditions for his synthesis not within the text but without – a *nothing* to the apes – because a *thing* – 'It cannot be *a genius!*'[60]

In previous commentaries, the mutually assured destruction that ensues when these two rival bearers of the sacred word go head to head in the chapter 'Lord Osmund's Lenten Party', is often taken to indicate that whatever Pierpoint had planned is somehow turning awry. 'Whatever Pierpoint's beliefs and intentions, his campaign against the apes he identifies in his Encyclical is waged through unreliable lieutenants', states Edwards. 'Two of them ... are capable of parroting at great length and with great conviction Pierpoint's Lewisian analyses of the art world ... but they ruin the show at Lord Osmund's party by squabbling over unpaid bills in public.'[61] Similar criticism is levelled at Lewis's other great novel from this period, *The Childermass* (1928), in which another actor and magician, possessed of transformative powers, squares off against another Welshman and Fascist, in a refugee-camp outside Heaven. After considerable fanfare, the long promised battle for reality seems about to begin when the latter faction secure a platform; but rather than 'showing up' the 'Bailiff', exposing the magic tricks and misconceptions that underpin his rule, these 'Hyperideans' come to realize that they are in agreement with their enemy's philosophy or that their key ideas have been stolen by him and are already being implemented (in what must count as an early example of 'triangulation'). Their conclusion: 'What a pity that you are in charge!'[62]

In contrast, the theoretical framework set out in this essay for the evaluation of Lewis's great period must suggest that these scenes represent in each case a successful outcome for the only participant of any consequence, the Ideal Giant. To suggest that either the apes' saturnalia or the parliament of the dead 'should be an epiphany', as previous commentators have suggested, is to miss

the point of the dialectical process Lewis took from Stirner.[63] 'It
was my idea at the outset', Lewis recalled of *The Art of Being Ruled*,
'inspired by the Hegelian dialectic, with its thesis and antithesis –
to state, here and there, both sides of the question to be debated,
and allow those opposites to struggle in the reader's mind for the
ascendancy and there to find their synthesis'.[64] No epiphany is viable
inside a work of art for the reason stated in Lewis's novel *Tarr* (1928):

> Deadness is the first condition for art: the second is absence of soul,
> in the human and sentimental sense … no restless inflammable
> ego is imagined for its interior: it has *no inside*: good art must have
> no inside: that is capital.[65]

Having demonstrated that naïve egotism or chauvinism in the
contemporary use of that term is not that 'one synthetic and various
ego' that comprises self and the not-self, we are now in a position
to perceive that a signal victory is neither possible nor even desired
for those things in himself that Lewis fixed upon as his 'most
essential ME'.[66] The Stirnerian dialectical method is not essentialist
but nihilist: aims not at restoration, but negation of negation.
The climactic moment that Starr-Smith disrupts could never have
been an epiphany because the God that 'always desires to manifest
himself' is not, as Edwards seems to suggest in his discussion of this
passage, Lewis's God, but a natural rather than artificial power, the
God of the magician rather than the artist, making itself visible here
in the only way it ever can: by disappearing the Subject. That is the
negation being negated: no epiphany from the magician or Shaman,
but a series of vanishing tricks. '[All] magicians dislike permanence,
and are naturally sympathetic towards the flux', states Lewis in *Time*

and *Western Man*. 'For operations involving *disappearances* are their *métier*. Nearly all their tricks are *vanishing tricks*.'[67]

The comedians

The Vanish in *The Apes of God* may be taken as the satiric counterpart to the historical process that Lewis had already charted in *Time and Western Man*, tracking the ego, 'briefly, from where we find it fully substantival at the opening of the great period of democratic stir and ferment in Europe, down to the time of its death in "action", of recent date'.[68] Having insisted that art is the civilized substitute for magic, Lewis accuses contemporaries of wishing to lead us back, 'by means of art, to the plane of magic, or of mystical, specifically religious, experience'. Instead of embracing the new possibilities presented by artist and scientist in the modern phase of European history, philosophers and cultural critics seek only 'to retransform both of them into the primitive magician from which they both equally spring, or rather to retransform their chosen material into simple magic'.[69]

Lewis's understanding of the dangers posed by this reversion to shamanism remains distinctively Stirnerian through the interwar years. The impetus behind *The Art of Being Ruled* is, Lewis claims at the outset, his desire to explode what Stirner terms *causes*, the category of *ideas* that empty out the individual subject, so that the latter becomes nothing but *a walking idea*. 'Dying for a idea' sounds well enough, writes Lewis, but why not let the idea die instead of you.[70] The book is a diatribe against any word that makes us strangers to ourselves, installing 'a principle of impersonality in the heart of our life that is anti-vital'.[71] The final section concludes with an echo of Stirner's contention that our heads remain 'haunted' by that most oppressive 'spook' – Man.[72] 'Our minds are still haunted by that Abstract Man', Lewis writes, 'that enlightened abstraction of a common humanity, which had its greatest advertisement in the eighteenth century'.[73]

But new ideas and points of reference increasingly complicate this Stirnerian base. In the course of his discussion of Schopenhauer, for instance, Lewis notes that the philosopher defends the 'self' from a predatory abstract idealism, but insists 'the individual should be kept in the most unequivocal subordination to his conception of the Will'.[74] In *Time and Western Man*, the individual subject is threatened not, or not primarily, by the Idea, but by this radical new empirical basis for Natural Science. Over the course of a chapter titled 'The Subject as King of the Psychological World', Lewis traces the evolution of the *unconscious mind* from its roots in the debates of Locke and Leibniz, over the Cartesian statement that '*the soul, as a thinking being, must think incessantly*', through to the *élan vital* of Bergson and the *Radical Empiricism* of William James. 'So it is that *the Subject* is not gently reasoned out of, but violently hounded from every cell of the organism: until at last (arguing that "independent", individual life is not worthwhile, nor the game worth the candle) he plunges into the *Unconscious*', Lewis concludes – 'where Dr. Freud, like a sort of mephistophelian Dr. Caligari, is waiting for him'.[75] In another chapter, Lewis even goes so far as to suggest that 'Realist' and 'Idealist' can no longer be said to differ in any significant respect.[76]

In a startling twist to the Stirnerian historical schema, the rise of the artist and the scientist is shown to have brought about a very different synthesis to that predicted by Stirner. No *Ideal Giant* (the future of the artist has not materialized) but an *Ideal Comedian*: 'In dealing with the question of the *sense of personal identity*, James says that our belief that the *Me* of yesterday is the same as the Me of today is "a mere subjective phenomenon"', states Lewis.[77] And the Comedian, in the picture of these many distinct, intermittent selves, finds his professional paradise. 'For all comedians are necessarily volatile, love change for change's sake, prefer parasitically other personalities and other lives to their own – such is their faculty and function: they would desire never twice to be the same thing: to have at their disposal an infinite number of masks.'[78] In politics, the Ideal Comedian is said to manifest as a type of Mussolini: 'with all the instincts bred behind the footlights, the apotheosis of the life-of-the-moment, of exteriority, display and make-up; and of an extreme instability, fundamental breaks and intermittences, the natural result of the violent changes of, and the return of great chaotic violences into, our time'. In the arts, continues Lewis, this tendency issues in the form of prodigious virtuosity. 'The work of one person will consist of the schematic juxtaposition of a series of disconnected stylizations; and therefore, since the "style is the man", of a crowd of men, not one man at all. So the co-existence is achieved of many persons and times in one.'[79]

Much of Lewis's fictional and critical output in the interwar period is devoted to the exposure of these *Ideal Comedians*, and perhaps the most vicious of these personal attacks is the 'Analysis of the Mind of James Joyce' in *Time and Western Man*. By far the best known and most widely quoted of Lewis's polemical work, this piece acquires a new significance within the theoretical context established by this essay. In this light it is clear that Joyce is guilty, not merely of reiterating like Gertrude Stein the radical empiricism of William James, nor like Ezra Pound, of simply failing to understand the wider implications of his creative practice (a 'Revolutionary Simpleton'). The vitriol directed at Joyce can now be understood to stem from Lewis's (perhaps mistaken) perception that *Ulysses* had enacted precisely that thought-experiment we find in his own work (stating, here and there, both sides of the question to be debated, allowing opposites to struggle in the reader's mind for the ascendancy – there to find their synthesis) – but had then arrived at a markedly different result. As in *The Childermass*, a Celt with an improbable Greek name, representing a Classical or spatial mind-set, goes head to head with a Jew, embodying what Lewis called a *time-mind*. But though 'urged by his author to rise to the occasion and live up to the role of the incarnation of the immaterial, and so be top-dog to Poldy Bloom', Stephen Dedalus simply will not grow into 'the protagonist of a battle between mighty principles of Spirit and Matter'.[80] Having disavowed this portrait of himself as a young man, the author, 'thinly disguised as a middle-aged Jew tout (Mr Leopold Bloom)', is said to win the reader's sympathy every time he appears; 'is never confronted with the less and less satisfactory Dedalus (in the beau role) without the latter losing trick after trick to his disreputable rival; and so, to the dismay of the conscientious reader, betraying the principles he represents'. Lewis concludes that 'It is a sad affair, altogether, on that side.'[81] In a critique that foreshadows the existential psychology of schizophrenia developed by R.D. Laing, Lewis argues that ego must inevitably collapse in the face of the (radical empiricist) psychological method, the immense *nature-morte* that must result; 'a ton or two of personally organised rubbish'.[82] As Lewis had predicted in *The Caliph's Design* (1919), the human had been overwhelmed by its own creation (or as he put it in *BLAST*, the fraternal moulds that attract modern town-dwellers): 'The danger, as it would appear at present, and in our first flight of substitution and remounting, is evidently that we should become overpowered by our creation, and become as mechanical as a tremendous insect world, all our awakened reason [that distinguishes the third phase in the Lewisian schematic history – the time of the New Ego, of the Artist] entirely disappeared.'[83]

Lewis's frustration at Joyce's perversion (as he perceived it) of the dialectical form he had developed in 'Enemy of the Stars' can only have been compounded by his knowledge of the extent to which this fellow Man-of-1914 had grounded his creative project on Stirnerian egoism. Both had been published in *The Egoist* by Dora Marsden, and as Bruce Clarke has shown in his book on the editor, in Joyce's case at least, this was because *A Portrait of the Artist as a Young Man* realized her vision of a literature that would constitute a psychology of egoism. Joyce cites Stirner as a major influence on his thought in a note to his biographer Herbert Gorman, and the philosopher's influence is pervasive in this first novel, which can be seen to conform closely to that step-by-step account of a typical individual's psychological development set out in the first chapter of *The Ego and His Own*.[84] Like Stirner's egoist, Stephen Dedalus passes on from an initial phase in which he is subject to physical tyrannies of family and school, only then to fall under the spiritual dominion of the Church. Having freed himself from the latter, Stephen must resist its humanitarian reiterations in order to achieve his goal: that is (like the Lewisian egoist) to become his own Artist. Earlier versions of the

Portrait can be seen to draw yet more heavily on Stirnerian theory – as Jean-Michel Rabaté has recently demonstrated. 'It was part of that ineradicable egoism which he was afterwards to call redeemer', writes Joyce, 'that he imagined converging to him all the deeds and thoughts of the microcosm'.[85] And in Rabaté's opinion, 'This thought cannot simply be ascribed to youthful enthusiasm, since we find it in Stephen's mouth at the close of *Ulysses*, in "Eumaeus", when Stephen declares to a baffled Bloom 'that Ireland must be important because it belongs to [him]'.[86]

In his Lacanian reading of Joyce's oeuvre, Rabaté argues that the move towards the decentred subjectivity one encounters in *Finnegans Wake* does not represent the rejection of Stirnerian egoism for a radical empiricism, but the culmination of the former through the latter. In Stirner's philosophy, the ego as posited (or in Lewisian terms, the persona) insofar as it possesses existence, is appearance, and is essence (that is to say, is the creator of a persona thus posited) only insofar as it does not exist. And from the earliest versions of *A Portrait*, Joyce had conflated ego with negation in a pun that can be understood to have anticipated everything that would follow in the Wake: 'His "Nego ... written amid a chorus of peddling Jews" gibberish and Gentile clamour', writes Joyce, 'was drawn up valiantly while true believers prophesied fried atheism and was hurled against the obscene hells of our Holy Mother'.[87] In that picture of many distinct intermittent selves we find in the *Wake*, we should perceive, not disintegration of ego, but multiplication: 'a grammar of egoism – in which the active and passive voices keep revolving around a mobile subjective center'.[88] For Rabaté, this lability of the 'I' is derived from the key property of a Stirnerian Unique who is also *causa sui*. 'Throughout his career, the strategy adopted by Joyce will remain the same: by hiding under the tables of the Law, he multiplies his "I's" in order to avoid the frightening beaks.' In the *Wake* – as in Freud's *Interpretation of Dreams* – ego is represented several times over and in various forms because – in the view of both Joyce and Freud – 'Dreams are completely egotistical'.[89]

A Lewisian reading of the Joycean dream-work must be at one with Lacan on this score: no work of art that does not result from the free action of a living Subject. To accept Rabaté's interpretation of Joyce's work, as sharing a common basis in the egoist philosophy of Max Stirner, is to acquire a new understanding of the Lewisian critique as a sectarian action. The specific thrust of the argument is more precise once it is recognized that the Joycean dream-work is not an alien system of thought, that Lewis is gunning not for an enemy without but within. A purge, a pogrom; this dispute is fraternal, taking issue not with the fundamental beliefs underpinning the creation of *Finnegans Wake*, but with their application. Lewis resists the suggestion, advanced again later in the century by Deleuze and Guattari, that there is radical potential in this egalitarian dispersal of the Subject; that is to say, in a failure to distinguish between that which is your *self* and that which is your *own* (properties of the ego) on the part of the schizophrenic, or *Schizoid*.

Funerary art

In the rigorous steps to police this distinction introduced in *The Childermass* and *The Apes of God* we have seen that Lewis presents a compelling alternative to a radical subjectivity often taken to represent the mainstream of Modernism (and typically attributed to the radical empiricism of James and Bergson). In closing, I would like to point out problems inherent in the dialectical procedure developed by Lewis. In eliminating the confusion of self and property that entangles Arghol in 'The Enemy of the Stars', Lewis inevitably projects into the work an essential ME – a portrait of the artist – perhaps less like the one synthetic and various ego that created the work than the Domestic Adversary – the shamans or magicians that possess that transformative energy proper to the artist in every living thing.

In what is perhaps the most extraordinary scene in Lewis's *The Childermass*, his answer to *Finnegans Wake*, the Bailiff is seen to sink back in a painting that serves as the backcloth to his booth, merging in the form of the divinity depicted there: the adolescent god of Thrace, with leopard-skin and thyrsus, worshipped in the Orphic Mysteries: 'The Thracian divinity skoal-drinks with dashing nordic abandon then crashes the goblet down bottom-up, true Thracian-Norse, upon the shelf before him.'[90] In stark contrast, that faithful portrait of the Artist, Hyperides, though likened in appearance to Michelangelo, is immobile, inert. Bound to support a Lewisian line on art, he is required to *communicate* a vision that is diametrically opposed to everything he *is*: 'stretched out in the relaxed repose of the Sistine Adam [his] finger points inertly forward as though waiting the touch of the hurrying Jehovah.'[91] In preventing an indiscriminate confusion of self and world, Lewis inevitably *appears* to have relinquished the mercurial properties of the living ego that make art possible. If Joyce is taken to represent a pantheistic dispersal, blurring into the contours of his dream landscape, present in every river, tree and hill,

Lewis is (to paraphrase W.H. Auden) too easily taken for *that lonely volcano on the right*... ('The mountains were an idea of mine!' says the Bailiff. 'They are as a matter of fact from Iceland, volcanic as you see I daresay – that is the Skapta Jokul...'[92])

And perhaps this is no mistake. In his pre-war writing Lewis had identified himself to a greater or lesser degree with the final stage in Stirner's evolution; his shamanic figures from the North, Kerr-Orr and Arghol, had struggled against or tried to accommodate those bullet-like egos encountered where Africa begins. In the post-war writing, Lewis took issue with the resulting synthesis and fought for Ideal Giant against Ideal Comedian. Hurling his weight behind the Thracian or Phrygian horsemen that first shattered the shamanic/orphic system of sex-magic in ancient Bulgaria, Lewis championed the Lion over the Fox, in order to secure a result like the Greek synthesis or Italian renaissance. But whatever synthesis this author envisaged happening *outside the text* must necessarily remain just that, happening only if the reader takes the considerable time and effort to make it happen. And unfortunately, what readers *actually* encounter in Lewis's writing, until the thirties at least, is precisely that inertness (that fixity, that mortmain) now associated with the art produced under *fascism*. The opening sequence in Leni Riefenstahl's *Olympia* (1938); those unmoving tableaus, 'like a spirited salon-picture', that Lewis ridiculed in Pound's 'Canto XVII'; the six characters in search of an author, in the play of that name by Luigi Pirandello. This material history is no less dead – no less a *nature-morte* – for being said to follow on, rather than constitute, the passage through time of an ego – our *Angelus Novus*, the artist.

4

A NEW CONCEPT
OF EGOISM

The Late-Modernism of Ayn Rand

'It stood on the edge of the Boston Post Road, two small structures of
glass and concrete forming a semicircle among the trees: the cylinder
of the office and the long, low oval of the diner, with gasoline pumps
as the colonnade of a forecourt between them.'[1] The writer goes on to
describe this Modernist petrol station in terms that recall the rapture
of Marinetti, describing the car-crash that launched Futurism; or
that of Le Corbusier, encountering the titanic reawakening of
Parisian traffic that led him to develop his Voisin Plan, a new
approach to urban-planning formulated specifically in order to
facilitate a free movement of automobiles. 'It looked like a cluster
of bubbles hanging low over the ground, not quite touching it, to be
swept aside in an instant on a wind of speed; it looked gay, with the
hard, bracing gaiety of efficiency, like a powerful airplane engine.'[2]

But this building is designed neither by Mies van der Rohe nor
Arne Jacobsen. It is the creation of Howard Roark, hero of Ayn
Rand's novel *The Fountainhead* (1943) – and it is worth underlining

how strange this ought to seem. A declared Romantic (who favoured Victor Hugo over the sort of innovators who never used capitals, never used commas and wrote poems that neither rhymed nor scanned) Rand must appear an unlikely champion of Modernism in architecture. Indeed, Rand's egoist philosophy presents a perfect example of that mistrust of grand narrative now thought to be central to the 'cultural logic of late-capitalism', post-modernism. In place of 'all the variants of modern collectivism (communist, fascist, Nazi, etc.), which preserve the religious-altruist ethics in full and merely substitute "society" for God as the beneficiary of man's self-immolation', Rand proposes a new social order geared to the individual: 'a free, productive, rational system that rewards the best in every man, and which is, [as Frederic Jameson rather feared it might be] obviously, laissez-faire capitalism'.[3]

In fact, Rand's philosophy has had a role equal or greater than that of Milton Friedman or F.A. Hayek in shaping a contemporary neo-liberal consensus, having had an avowed impact upon theorists such as George Gilder, whose *Wealth and Poverty* (1981) has been called the 'bible' of the Reagan administration, and Charles Murray, who launched an early, influential attack on the welfare-state in *Losing Ground* (1984). Rand's philosophy is regularly cited as an inspiration by a new breed of industrialists based in California's Silicon Valley, where the IT and business-models that powered the neo-liberal experiment were first developed. Influential public figures on the American right, Rush Limbaugh, Rick Santelli, Paul Ryan, Rand Paul and Donald Trump are admirers of Rand's work. And Alan Greenspan, Chairman of the US Federal Reserve between 1987 and

2006, and perhaps the primary architect of our highly deregulated and globalized financial order is her protégé.[4]

And yet, there is clearly no discrepancy between Roark's Modernist practice and his 'post-modernist' philosophy. The fact is that Rand presents readers with a total philosophy for living – in a period supposedly wary of the great Modernist passion for system building. 'Weary from Communism, fascism, and two world wars intellectuals were above all uninterested in ideology', writes Jennifer Burns in her biography *The Goddess of the Markets* (2009): 'Rand's Objectivism, a completely integrated rational, atheistic philosophical system delivered via a thousand-page novel, was simply not what most established intellectuals were looking for in 1957.'[5] No doubt one could argue Rand is a transitional figure in the great twentieth-century paradigm shift. Equally disregarding the extravagant claims made for her work by her acolytes and the blanket dismissal of ideological opponents, one might conceivably characterize Rand as a right-wing counterpart to Aldous Huxley: a resolutely middlebrow writer, who chose to apply ideas and techniques pioneered by Modernists without being of that movement, and again like Huxley (or Robert Graves) eventually to enjoy untimely success with the rise of a later generation, in the sixties. To some extent this is clearly correct. But, I suggest, this analogy only serves to underscore the inadequacy of the theoretical terms coined in that first, heroic attempt to describe theories and practices that had no place in what was then universally agreed to constitute the Modernist movement: neither in the (radical) empiricist tradition that inspired Marcel Proust's *La recherche du temps perdu* and Gertrude Stein's *The Making of Americans,* nor in the mainstream of (Hegelian) idealism, wherein one might place the inter-subjectivity of T.S. Eliot's *The Waste Land,* nor yet in any tradition representing the admixture of these, the cultural logic of late capitalism seemed to possess no obvious precedent: and was therefore declared to be post-Modernist. I suggest this is a mistake.

In this essay I propose to show that Rand's Objectivism must be recognized as a late Modernism: an untimely contribution to a body of discourse produced (for the most part) immediately prior to the First World War – which itself constituted a belated response to the insurrectionary egoist philosophy of the renegade Hegelian Max Stirner. Though the impact of Stirnerian egoism has been examined in the work of individual writers, sporadically, over the past four decades, by critics Michael Levenson, Bruce Clarke, John F. Welsh, and Jean-Michel Rabaté, these writers have never been considered together: and understood to constitute a Modernism possessing a philosophical basis distinct from that of the mainstreams. I argue that, through Ayn Rand primarily, the Modernism of radical subjectivity survived well beyond the point thought to mark its extinction post– First World War; that the cultural logic of late capitalism is based, to a significant degree, upon this Modernist interpretation of Stirnerian egoism. The political urgency of the reappraisal undertaken in this essay need hardly be spelt out. Endeavours to engage with a contemporary hyper-modernist transformation of our city-spaces, with the slow perversion of our social and economic systems, must remain ineffectual as long as an understanding of the cultural logic underpinning the grand 'neo-liberal' insurrection is distorted by a terminology as yet inexact.

The Fountainhead

Disavow the immediate past. The gesture is characteristically Modernist – and in this respect Howard Roark is entirely typical. 'I inherit nothing', he says. 'I stand at the end of no tradition. I may, perhaps, stand at the beginning of one.'[6] Rand, his creator, was to make similar claims. 'The only philosopher she acknowledged as an influence was Aristotle', writes her most recent biographer, Jennifer Burns. 'Beyond his works, Rand insisted that she was unaffected by external influences or ideas.'[7] Her oeuvre presents readers with what appears to be a self-enclosed system of thought; if Rand requires an authoritative opinion she will often cite one of her own fictional characters, as though these were real people. 'When I am questioned about myself', she wrote in 1945, 'I am tempted to say, paraphrasing Roark: "Don't ask me about my family, my childhood, my friends or my feelings. Ask me about the things I think".'[8] In the eyes of her many fans, Rand is a sort of phoenix, possessing no context save her own creativity, the fountainhead that produced the universe they inhabit, *ex nihilio.*

> It is the content of a person's brain, not the accidental details of his life, that determines his character. My own character is in the pages of *The Fountainhead*. For anyone who wishes to know me, that is essential. The specific events of my private life are of no importance whatever. I have never had any private life in the usual sense of the word. My writing is my life.[9]

As political scholar and libertarian theorist Chris Matthew Sciabarra remarks, Rand's self-portrait 'verges on the reification of her intellect as a disembodied abstraction and this is strange as Rand herself often paid close attention to context in her analysis of philosophical and cultural trends'.[10] In *Ayn Rand: The Russian Radical* (1995), Sciabarra suggests that an assessment of her philosophy cannot be complete without a contextual and developmental basis. 'Rand was notorious for maintaining that her intellectual debt to other thinkers was very limited. And yet in my own research, I discovered similarities between Rand's approach and the dialectical approach of Hegelians and Marxists.'[11] While noting that Rand would have denied such a link vehemently, Sciabarra believes that at some point in her intellectual development Rand had absorbed, perhaps unwittingly, crucial aspects of a specifically dialectical method of analysis: that is to say, the attempt to overcome formal dualism and monistic reductionism, to uncover assumptions shared by apparent opposites, to achieve a transcendent perspective that insists on the integrity of the whole. 'Rand's revolt against formal dualism is illustrated in her rejection of such "false alternatives" as materialism and idealism, intrinsicism and subjectivism, rationalism and empiricism', observes Sciabarra. 'Moreover, Rand always views the polarities as "mutually" or "reciprocally reinforcing," "two sides of the same coin".' According to Sciabarra, this is no mere technique. 'Rand was the first to admit that a writer's style is a product of his or her "psycho-epistemology" or method of awareness.'[12]

Sciabarra traces Hegelian elements in Ayn Rand's fiction and philosophy back to her time in St. Petersburg. His pioneering book was the first to suggest that Rand's studies in the years immediately following the Russian Revolution must be taken into account in any serious assessment of her philosophical work. During her time at the Stoiunin Gymnasium and later in the Department of Social Pedagogy at the University of Petrograd, Rand would have encountered the most highly regarded Hegelians of that era, the most significant of these being N.O. Lossky, who held a position in pre-First World War Russian philosophy comparable to that of his contemporary F.H. Bradley in England. Creator of a distinctively Russian variety of Hegelianism that fused Slavicist politics and mystical elements derived from Russian Orthodox tradition, Professor Lossky had lectured at the Stoiunin Gymnasium on Fichte, Hegel and Schelling in the years that Rand was a student there and, though the State Scientific Council had compelled him to retire from his university post in the year Rand enrolled, he might have provided unofficial tuition to students on the history of ancient thought. In conversations with her first biographer Barbara Branden, Rand described Lossky as a 'distinguished international authority on Plato' – though this was not his primary area of expertise – and recalled with pride that Lossky had praised her forthright rejection of Platonism.[13] The passage is suggestive, Sciabarra points out: the one teacher whose approval ever seems to have counted for anything with Rand, Lossky is not recognized as a Hegelian – so might be the means whereby Rand acquired a dialectical method of analysis without being aware that she was doing so. Sciabarra's theory has met with mixed responses. While biographer Jennifer Burns reserves judgement, another recent biographer, Anne C. Heller endorses Sciabarra, stating that Rand 'learned from Lossky an intensely dialectical method of thinking – "thinking in principles", she called it – which helped her to construct a worldview that was radically individualistic and seemingly Western but in some ways Russian to the core'.[14]

But Rand was far from short on teaching material that set out the background to historical materialism – and so one really has to question how Rand could have failed to recognize critical procedures taught by Lossky or other Hegelians at the university for what they were. In semi-autobiographical novel *We the Living* (1936), Rand lists the lectures her character Kira is forced to attend, satirizing the pro-Bolshevik nature of the material on the syllabus: 'Proletarian Women and Illiteracy', 'The Spirit of the Collective', 'Proletarian Electrification', 'The Doom of Capitalism', 'The Red Peasant', 'The ABC of Communism', 'Comrade Lenin and Comrade Marx' and 'Marx and Collectivism'.[15] Rand later complained that her university degree programme 'began with Plato, whom the regime claimed as the forerunner to historical materialism, then went to Hegel, then to Marx'.[16] 'For the rest of her life,' writes Barbara Branden, 'Alice knew that she understood the theory of dialectical materialism – and had on her body and spirit the scars of its practice – as few Americans would; she did not bear with equanimity the remarks of anyone who ventured to tell her "what communism really was all about" '.[17]

But if Rand *knew she understood* the theory of dialectical materialism one must really struggle to explain the paradox that is 'For the New Intellectual' (1960): an essay that performs the very 'triple somersaults' Rand ridicules in the moment she criticizes the 'plain Witch-doctory of Hegel'.[18] If not the result of ignorance nor bad faith, might this apparent discrepancy between the values expressed and procedures employed indicate that Rand's dialectical procedure was derived from a source she had good reason to regard as anti-Hegelian? The historical overview provided in 'For the New Intellectual' certainly bears an astonishing resemblance to that offered by renegade Hegelian Max Stirner in the second part of *Der Einzige und sein Eigentum*: that historical progression from 1) the initial tyranny of physical facts – through 2) the religious or ideological tyranny of shaman/priest/humanist – which finally culminates in 3) freedom for living ego.[19]

The three 'contestants' described in Rand's essay correspond to a specifically Stirnerian application of the dialectical method. First, there is *Attila*, 'the man who rules by brute force, acts on the range of the moment, is concerned with nothing but the physical reality immediately before him, respects nothing but man's muscles, and regards a fist, a club or a gun as the only answer to any problem.'[20] Next, *the Witch Doctor*, 'the man who dreads physical reality, dreads the necessity of practical action, and escapes into his emotions, into visions of some mystic realm where his wishes enjoy a supernatural power unlimited by the absolutes of nature.'[21] And though these two figures – the man of force and the man of faith – might appear to be opposites, they share 'a consciousness held down to the *perceptual* method of functioning', which Rand glosses as an 'awareness that does not choose to extend beyond the automatic, the immediate, the given, the involuntary, which means: an animal's "epistemology"'. According to Rand, 'Man's consciousness shares with animals the first two stages of its development: sensations and perceptions; but it is the third state, *conceptions*, that makes him man.'[22] As in the writings of Dora Marsden and Wyndham Lewis before her, Stirner's third stage in the history of mankind is identified with this capacity for integrating perceptions into conceptions by a process of abstraction; that is to say, reason or thought.[23] In Rand's philosophy, only an egoist can think for himself – can realize an innate potential for being human (a rational animal): 'while animals survive by adjusting themselves to their background, man survives by adjusting his background to himself'.[24] Like Marsden and Lewis, Rand stresses this capacity of the ego to transform that which is given into that which is its *own*: the man of reason, is *the Producer*.[25] And, like Marsden, Rand distinguishes between two categories – broadly corresponding to the traditional Sciences and Humanities. 'The professional businessman', argues Rand, 'is the field agent of the army whose commander-in-chief is the *scientist*', while 'The professional intellectual is the field agent of the army whose commander-in-chief is the *philosopher*.[26] And once again, the achievements of the first group are held up as a reproach to the latter, Rand suggesting (like Marsden some years earlier) that philosophers have proven either unwilling or incapable of moving beyond phase two.[27] 'His twin brother, the businessman, has done a superlative job and has brought men to an unprecedented material prosperity', concludes Rand. 'But the intellectual has sold him out – has betrayed their common source – has failed in his own job and has brought men to spiritual bankruptcy.[28] As in *Time and Western Man*, Idealist and Empiricist represent a relapse to earlier, non-rational modes of being – Witch Doctor and Attila, respectively – two 'false alternatives' persisting upon this second – more sophisticated – tier of the Stirnerian dialectic.[29]

We know for a fact that Rand and her immediate circle (who ironically called themselves The Collective) were familiar with Stirner by the sixties, as Nathaniel Branden mentions the philosopher (in the course of correcting a misconception that egoism is doing whatever one wants) in his essay 'Counterfeit Individualism' (1962): 'Nietzsche and Max Stirner', he writes, 'are sometimes quoted in support of this interpretation.'[30] But the reasoning behind this rejection of Nietzschean/Stirnerian egoism is entirely consistent with the way in which Stirner's thought had been developed earlier in the century by leading Modernist writers working within a Stirnerian framework. Lewis, for instance, condemns Henri Bergson in exactly the same terms in *Time and Western Man* – arguing that the emphasis placed upon the subconscious implies a subordination of the individual to some impersonal system that must compromise the integrity of the Self.[31] If we choose to take Stirnerian egoism in a wider sense – as a counterpart to Marxism, a living body of discourse, open to reinterpretation and modification, rather than a dead letter – the extent to which Rand's philosophy of rational self-interest differs from Stirner 'whim-worship' presents no fundamental obstacle to our regarding the former as an off-shoot of the latter, part of this one tradition/anti-tradition of radical thought.

Put simply, *The Ego and His Own* and 'For the New Intellectual' have far more in common than can pass for chance; and Rand's moral philosophy (the bedrock for her subsequent Capitalist politics and 'Objectivist' epistemology) possesses a peculiarly Stirnerian flavour too. 'The social theory of ethics substitutes "society" for God', states Rand, echoing Stirner's critique of early socialism, 'and although it claims that its chief concern is life on earth, it is *not* the life of man, not the life of an individual, but the life of a disembodied entity, *the collective*, which, in relation to every individual, consists of everybody except himself'.[32] The egoism that provided the initial impetus for Rand's project has sometimes been likened to that of Nietzsche, but the particular thrust of her attack, in passages like this from *The Virtue of Selfishness* (1964), is distinctly *Stirnerian* in form and content, is on occasion near word for word: 'since there is no such entity as "society"', Rand insists, 'since society is only a number of individual men – this means that some men (the majority or any gang that claims to be its spokesman) are ethically entitled to pursue and whims (or any atrocities) they desire to pursue, while *other* men are ethically obliged to spend their lives in the service of that gang's desires.'[33]

This (by now familiar) moral insight can also be seen to produce similar (and equally startling) political conclusions in the writings of both Stirner and Rand. Unlike his early Anarchist admirers, Stirner did not push for the abolition of the State, imagining that statism would inevitably wither away as more and more egoists opted to withdraw their creativity from the system, forming in its stead *the Union of Egoists* – a voluntary association, for a free trade in properties and powers, bound together only by the self-interest of each individual participant, a perpetual insurrection. Stirner was vague on how a Union might work, reserving the right to change his mind to suit himself. Having dispensed with this crucial liberty, Rand is more forthcoming – and, in the business community that retires to Galt's Gulch in *Atlas Shrugged* we have a fantasy that is closer than anything produced before or since to what Max Stirner may have meant. 'Here', Ellis Wyatt tells Dagney, 'we trade achievements, not failures – values, not needs. We're free of one another, yet we all grow together.'[34] Indeed, Rand's prime innovation consists in her recognition that Stirner's proposal for a bartering system without

State intervention is already there in the laissez-faire capitalism of Adam Smith. 'Capitalism is based on self-interest and self-esteem', wrote Greenspan in 1963; 'it holds holds integrity and trustworthiness as cardinal virtues and makes them pay off in the market-place, demanding that men survive by means of virtues, not of vices. It is this superlatively moral system that the welfare statists propose to improve on by means of preventive law, snooping bureaucrats, and the chronic goad of fear.'[35]

The house of dead truths

But how to account for these parallels? We have evidence to prove that Rand knew of Max Stirner by the beginning of the sixties – but is the influence of that philosopher merely a late development, or is it still possible to conclude that these unlikely 'Hegelian' components in Rand's system of thought were acquired far earlier, during her formative period, in Soviet Russia, as Sciabarra suggested? The available evidence would seem to suggest that Rand did not possess *first-hand* knowledge of Stirner until the sixties (and perhaps not even then). 'These are the vague beginnings of an amateur philosopher', writes Rand, in her 'First Philosophic Journal', on 9 April 1934. 'To be checked with what I learn when I master philosophy – then see how much of it has already been said, and whether I have anything new to say, or anything old to say better than it has already been said.'[36] Subsequent entries indicate that Rand worked through a reading-list consisting of some of the key radical right-wing texts of the era, but Stirner had again fallen into utter obscurity, and the only name that Rand could put to the body of ideas she had carried with her, on leaving Russia for the New World, remained that of Friedrich Nietzsche.

According to Barbara Branden, Rand first discovered this philosopher while at university, when a cousin said to her, grinning with a touch of malice, 'Here is someone you should read, because he beat you to all your ideas.' Intrigued, Rand began reading *Thus Spake Zarathustra*. In Nietzsche, Rand believed she had found a writer 'who felt as I did about man, who saw and wanted the heroic in man; here was a writer who believed that a man should have a great purpose, a purpose which is for his own sake, for his own happiness and his own selfish motives'.[37] His books would have a profound impact. 'The seventeen-year-old Rand immediately seized upon his ideas', writes Anne C. Heller, 'including his call to discard old values and create new ones, his condemnation of altruism as a slave morality, his argument for the inviolate rights of the gifted person, whose only obligation is to refine and use his gifts as he sees fit'.[38] From the first, Rand later claimed, Nietzsche's defence of psychological determinism had troubled her, and so too various statements concerning the exercise of power. 'I believed that the superior man could not be bothered enslaving others, that slavery is immoral, that to enslave his inferiors is an unworthy occupation for the heroic man.'[39] According to Barbara Branden, when Rand read further in Nietzsche and found in *The Birth of Tragedy* he was 'statedly anti-reason', her early enthusiasm began to abate. 'He said that reason is an inferior faculty', remembered Rand, 'that drunken-orgy emotions were superior. That finished him as a spiritual ally.'[40]

Rand is here somewhat misleading. It is precisely those aspects of Nietzschean thought she later professed to have immediately disliked which loom largest in her earliest fictional writing. In detailed plans for a novel to have been called 'The Little Street', Rand models her anti-social hero Denis Renehan on the child-murderer William Edward Hickman. Had this book ever been completed it would have resembled something approaching a cross between *The Outsider* by Albert Camus and Truman Capote's *In Cold Blood* – a supremely amoral modern novel that would have forever put its author into a very different category of American literature. Nietzschean elements persist in the original version of *We the Living* too. In a passage cut from later editions, a Communist called Andrei tells the hero Kira that he knows what she is going to say: she admires Bolshevik ideals, but loathes their methods. 'I loathe your ideals', Kira replies, 'I admire your methods. If one believes one's right, one shouldn't wait to convince millions of fools, one might just as well force them. I don't know, however, whether I'd include blood in my methods.'[41] Finally, early drafts for *The Fountainhead* indicate that Rand initially conceived of even her exemplary egoist-as-creator, Howard Roark as a Nietzschean Superman, an amoral force like Denis Renehan in 'The Little Street', or Lev Manovich in *We the Living*. (That is to say, rapist and terrorist.) Elements of this characterization persist in the finished novel: Roark (notoriously) remains a rapist, and, of course, ultimately dynamites a housing estate. But, fortunately, Nietzschean traces such as these are obscured by lyrical passages celebrating Rand's new (Stirnerian[42]) concept of egoism as rational self-interest. Though her contempt for the masses resurfaces to disastrous effect in *Atlas Shrugged*, it is this emphasis on the creative potential of the individual, together with her celebration of loving and resilient social-networks (as creators unite to work on projects such as the Stoddard Temple) for which Rand is best remembered.

Having noted that there are these Nietzschean elements in Rand's early fiction is it possible to accept these represent a distortion of a pre-existing egoism? Rand insists that this is the case, but suggests that this insight was personal and owed nothing to education or environment: for how could an egoist owe anything to a land as unrelentingly hostile to the individual as Russia? 'My feeling toward Russia [is] simply an intensified feeling that I've had from childhood and from before the revolutions', Rand recalled. 'I felt that this was so mystical, depraved, rotten a country that I wasn't surprised that they got a Communist ideology, and I felt that one has to get out and find the civilized world.'[43]

In Thomas Masaryk's classic history *The Spirit of Russia* (1919) we find that subjectivism was resisted, fiercely in fact, by a vast majority of Russian thinkers through the nineteenth century: but, significantly, this subjectivism 'was looked upon chiefly as the doctrine of Stirner'.[44] Aleksei Homjakov, Vissarion Grigorevic Belinsky, Aleksandr Herzen, Mikhail Bakunin, Dmitry Pisarev, Fyodor Dostoevsky, some of the greatest writers in the extraordinary renaissance that took place in Russia during the latter half of the nineteenth century, were struggling with a specifically Stirnerian variety of subjectivity. Neither Europe nor the United States could have presented a young woman with greater scope for encountering something of Stirner at secondhand. We know Rand read novels by Dostoevsky, for instance, presenting inversions, in her own work, of arguments derived from that novelist's denunciation of egoism in *Brothers Karamazov* (1880).

'For a long time, I studied his plots carefully', she told B. Branden, 'to see how he integrated his plots to his ideas.'[45] And in the nihilist philosophy of Pisarev, Rand would have found (had she cared to look) an interpretation of Stirner that anticipated her own much-vaunted emphasis upon a *rational* egoism. 'He preached radical individualism', writes Masaryk, 'understanding by this term the struggle for the emancipation of the individuality, a struggle that for him embodied the essential meaning of civilization.'[46] Towards the end of his great survey of Russian thought, Masaryk would note the increasing influence of Stirnerian egoism on anarchist thinkers in particular at the time he was writing (the First World War). 'The already great vogue of Nietzsche, Stirner and Ibsen continually increases... A number of recent writers have adopted anarchist views under the influence of these and other European exemplars. I may refer to F. Sologub with his solipsist paroxysms; and to L. Sestov, an imitator of Stirner and Nietzsche ...'[47]

This state of affairs in the period preceding the revolution has been obscured by Soviet propaganda. 'Consult any history of the Russian avant-garde', Allan Antliff observes, 'and you read that the artistic left pledged allegiance to the "October Revolution", i.e. the Communist Party coup of 1917 and subsequent dictatorship.'[48] As he and Nina Gurianova have discovered, in groundbreaking studies of anarchy and art, what this narrative misrepresents is a 'messy history' of artistic rebellion on the part of many in the Russian avant-garde in the first years of the Revolution: 'when anarchism, not Marxism, was the raison d'etre of their art'.[49] As Masaryk could have told us, the years between 1917 and 1919 were in fact the third in a series of three waves in the history of Russian political anarchism. The first of these in the 1870s produced a wide spectrum of different types of anarchism (e.g. the anarcho-christianity of Leo Tolstoy). The next took place between 1905 and 1907, during the first of the revolutions against the Tsarist regime. And significantly, according to Gurianova, 'The situation at the beginning of the century helped to promote different forms of anarcho-individualism, rather than anarcho-syndicalism or anarcho-communism.'[50] This final wave of insurrection happened to coincide with the publication of *six* translations of Stirner's book (between 1906 and 1910).[51] As a direct result, an anarcho-individualist sensibility emerged in Russia, which drew heavily upon the writing of Max Stirner.

In his presentation of Russian anarchist tendencies at the International Anarchist Congress in 1907, for instance, anarcho-communist Vladimir Ivanovich Zabrezhnev (Fedorov) singled out Stirner's philosophy for criticism, observing that the philosophy was proving popular – not with the factory-workers and revolutionary youth – but with an intelligentsia that 'tried to keep away from revolution'. According to Fedorov, these Russians 'naturally preferred Stirner's ideas and contradictory theory, [because these] allow any arbitrary conclusions'. He concluded these groups had no knowledge or understanding of anarchism as an integral philosophy: 'anarcho-individualists, Mystical Anarchists and … sexual perverts grow out of Stirner's ideas'.[52] Unhappily for Fedorov, these ideas would in fact provide the next generation of Russian Modernists with their ideological motivation. Though not widespread in Russia, individualist-anarchism possessed an intense appeal throughout the early twentieth century in the great metropolitan centres for the small circles of writers and artists that constituted the 'intelligentsia.'[53] In 1913, Ivan Ignatiev, for instance, became chairman of the Intuitive Association of Ego-Futurism, a group that included poets such as Vasilik Gnedov, Shirokov and Dmitry Kriuchkov. 'He used wordplay to name the group, in allusion to the most recent psychoanalyticalic concept of "ego", and after Max Stirner's individualist hero of *Der Einzige und sein Eigentum* (*The Ego and Its Own*), a book that had an immense influence on Russian culture, from Apollon Griegoriev and Dostoevsky to the Futurists', explains Gurianova. 'Ignatiev and Gnedov made direct references to anarcho-individualist ideas in their writings, for example, in Ignatiev's manifesto "Ego-Futurism", he praises Ego-Futurism as *egovyi* anarchism.'[54]

Such groups would acquire greater prominence with the last and strongest period of anarchist revival that began in 1917. While charismatic Nestor Makhno fought under the Black Flag in the Ukraine, on multiple fronts, against White and Red, the Moscow Federation of Anarchists was running twenty-five anarchist clubs across the capital, and distributing rifles, pistols and grenades to a militia known as the 'Black Guard'.[55] According to Antliff, these clubs were more than meeting-places; they were radical cultural institutions. 'For example, the "Dom Anarkhiia" (House of Anarchy), where the federation's official paper *Anarkhiia* was published, also featured a library and reading room, "proletarian art printing" facilities, a poetry circle, and a large theater hall in which plays were performed and lectures held.'[56] The radical writers and artists that frequented these clubs include many of the most significant names in the period, including painter Aleksandr Rodchenko, Kazimir Malevich (the leader of the Suprematist

school of painters), sculptor Vladimir Tatlin, and poets Vladimir
Mayakovsky and Vasili Kamensky.

In the present context 'Rodchenko's System' is of particular interest.
An effort to upstage Malevich and Tatlin, Rodchenko wrote this
manifesto to accompany a series of paintings called *Black on Black*
(1919). Rejecting the transcendental ego posited by Suprematism
as merely another iteration of that mystical abstraction (or 'spook')
Humanity, Rodchenko insisted upon an ego that would be a nothing,
perpetually negating each new affirmation of his own from moment
to moment. As we will see, it is in fact on this point that Rand breaks
with Stirner and with previous Modernist writers in this 'Stirnerian'
tradition. In a document that opens with passages from *Der Einzige
und sein Eigentum*, Rodchenko announced that the downfall of all
'isms' in painting must mark the beginning of his ascent. Note that
the artist insists on Stirnerian *analysis* rather than Hegelian *synthesis*
as the motive power of individual creativity:

> To the sound of the funeral bells of color painting, the last 'ism' is
> accompanied on its way to eternal peace, the last love and hope
> collapse, and I leave the house of dead truths. The motive power is
> not synthesis but invention (analysis). Painting is the body; creativity,
> the spirit.... I am the inventor of new discoveries in painting.[57]

Second-hand Rand

Is there evidence to suggest that Rand engaged with this extraordinary
moment of Stirnerian anarcho-individualism in politics and art?
Rand is known to have joined an underground network of writers'

clubs in St. Peterburg, participating in a subversive discourse that drew heavily on these theories. Heller notes that Rand never publicly acknowledged the influences that seem to enter the writing she produced at this time, but that these are evident nonetheless – 'stories and novel of a few then-famous Russian futurist and surrealist [sic] writers who lived in St. Petersburg in the early 1920s and made their names by envisioning the utopian, and anti-utopian, potential of the decade's new machines'.[58] Rand makes (rather vague) reference to this Modernist material in interviews with Barbara Branden thirty years later. 'There were a couple of modern novels by Russian writers that were semi-anti-Soviet or thinly veiled anti-Soviet that I liked for that reason, but that was minor', she insisted. 'I don't even remember the authors' names.'[59] While most accept this dismissal, Heller notes that Rand's sci-fi novel *Anthem* (1938) 'clearly reflects their influence'.[60]

Rand would recall she got the idea for this book in her school days, 'in Soviet Russia, when [she] heard all the vicious attacks on individualism, and asked [herself] what the world would be like if men lost the word"I"'.[61] Though Soviet Russia is only credited with raising the question, Branden hints that Futurist Russia offered her the answer. In her official biography (based for the most part upon recorded conversations with Rand) Barbara Branden remarks that the idea of projecting such a dystopian society was not new, being part of the intellectual ferment of the twenties. 'Yevgeny Zamyatin wrote his novel *We* in 1920–1921: it could not be published in Soviet Russia but was read to writers' groups and widely discussed throughout Petrograd.'[62] Though published in English in 1924, the book was not nearly as famous as it has became in the years since

Branden published her biography: and so it is quite possible that this final obscure detail relating to how writing was circulated (through *Samizdat*) during the Soviet era is taken from Rand. In any event, the parallels are indeed striking and pervasive.

Each book consists of a series of diary-entries presenting readers with a future in which individualism is eradicated and there is only a collective: a totalitarian society where deviance is punished by death. In each case the story hinges upon a moment of crisis when the altruism that hold the society together is threatened by a resurgent egoism: the writer of each journal has begun to love a specific woman above the all, thereby reactivating an 'atavistic' ego that can never again be at one with the rest. In the context of this essay, the single most interesting parallel between the stories of D-503 and Equality 7–2521 is the representation of socialism in Stirnerian terms, as merely the reiteration of Christian altruism, part of the spiritual (or Shamanist) phase in the history of humanity's moral development. D-503 recognizes that his society is based on an idea 'understood by the Christians, our only (if very imperfect) predecessors: Humility is a virtue, pride a vice; *We* comes from God, *I* from the devil'.[63] And this insight is reflected in the religious language Equality 7–2521 adopts in the early pages of his journal. 'By the grace of our brothers are we allowed our lives. We exist through, by and for our brothers who are the State. Amen.'[64]

But as Shoshana Milgram points out, the many similarities between *We* and *Anthem* (such as the regimentation of life, the world-wide state, the replacement of names by numbers, and the first-person narrative by a rebellious protagonist) provide no basis for assuming a causal relationship. There is nothing in *Anthem* that

Rand could not have taken from half-a-dozen utopias in circulation during the twenties. (Many of these actually put into print by Zamyatin while working as an editor for the World Literature Publishing House.[65]) As Milgram points out, the moral purpose underpinning the two Russian texts is not especially unusual either, but pervasive in work of writers who did not immediately follow the path of proletarian culture. Writers such as poet Vladimir Mayakovsky, for instance, expressed contempt for a proletarian school that believed it could achieve a new collectivism by effecting the abolition of the 'I'.

> The Proletcultists never speak
> of 'I'
> or of the personality.
> They consider
> the pronoun 'I'
> a kind of rascality . . . .
> But in my opinion
> if you write petty stuff, you
> will never crawl out of your lyrical slough
> even if you substitute We for I.[66]

Shoshana Milgram is clearly right to suggest that there is no case for insisting upon a causal relationship between *We* and *Anthem*: and for the matter in hand this hardly matters. The evidence compiled by Randian scholars for and against has simply served to underline one hugely significant point. That Rand was a product, typical in every respect, of this specific time and place, an intellectual milieu saturated by radical subjectivity. It is now possible to understand how a precocious undergraduate might have come to assimilate the key premises and methodological procedures at *second-hand* never knowing of their provenance. The writing of Ayn Rand can now be recognized as a belated contribution to that extraordinary moment in the history of First Wave Modernism when writers and artists across Europe explored the creative and political potential of Stirnerian insurrection.

2+2=4?

This new context must subtly alter a sense of the nature of Rand's achievement. As we have seen, Rand believed that the thing that put her work in a place apart from previous writing in the individualist tradition was the emphasis placed on reason. 'The advocacy of individualism as such is not new', writes Nathaniel Branden in 'Counterfeit Individualism'. What is new is the definition of an individualist as a man who lives not merely for his own sake but *by his own mind*. 'An individualist is, first and foremost, a *man of reason*.'[67] And this assessment of the Objectivist contribution to individualism appears particularly self-evident in those critical pieces that consider *Anthem* in relation to the nineteenth and twentieth century history of the literary utopia.

By far the most comprehensive evaluation of this kind is that of Shoshana Milgram, who compares Rand's novel to Fyodor Dostoevsky's *Notes from Underground*, H.G. Wells's *The Time Machine*, *The Sleeper Wakes*, *A Modern Utopia*, John W. Campbell's 'Twilight', E.M. Forster's 'The Machine Stops', Yevgeny Zamyatin's

We, Aldous Huxley's *Brave New World*, Stephen Benet's 'The Place of the Gods', and George Orwell's *1984*. In this context the rationalist turn highlighted by Nathaniel Branden, the break with 'irrational' forms of egoism, is unarguably the most distinctive aspect of Rand's intervention. For her work emerges as the first to challenge the conviction that the future most to be feared is the tyranny of Reason. The city of glass in Zamyatin, for instance, 'this extremely transparent and permanent crystal', is an imaginative projection of the Crystal Palace described by Dostoevsky; the regimentation of One-State makes real the possibility of a 'mathematical table' to regulate desires imagined by the Underground Man.[68] But as Heller points out, 'Rand concluded – long before most others – that totalitarianism *doesn't* work, because the independent motivation indispensable to economic and social progress cannot survive in an atmosphere of intimidation, coercion, and lack of individually earned rewards.'[69] Consequently, the collective in Rand's *Anthem* neither live in crystalline housing complexes nor manufacture anything like D-503's interstellar rocket-ship (called the INTEGRAL). The abolition of the 'I' is instead shown to have resulted in a physical as well as spiritual degradation. The candle is the most sophisticated invention to have been produced by her Committee of Scholars – and this is said to have taken fifty years. Milgram concludes that where the Underground Man had turned on mathematics as the fundamental quality of the Crystal Palace at which he wished to hurl stones, Rand rejects this unwarranted assault on reason and technology: 'reason is an individual act, a volitional act, and is thus anything but the enemy of freedom'.[70] In line with this shift, Rand imagines that individual rebellion against any form of collective oppression must necessarily manifest itself in thinking for oneself, rather than being driven by subconscious impulses. In *Notes from Underground*, the narrator asks, 'What do the laws of nature and arithmetic have to do with me, if for some reason, I don't happen to like those laws and that twice two is four?'[71] In *Atlas Shrugged*, Galt replies, 'the noblest act you have ever performed is the act of your mind in the process of grasping that two and two make four'.[72]

But what remains a seismic shift within the genre of utopian fiction is nothing of the sort within the context of egoism more generally, where this move towards reason had been anticipated by a series of Modernists working on the Stirnerian basis that Rand herself either began with or later adopted. Dmitry Pisarev, Dora Marsden, James Joyce, Wyndham Lewis – had all promoted the idea that selfhood requires the practice of reason; the latter two had even attempted something resembling that peculiar fusion of egoism and Aristotelian Thomism that Rand took such particular pride in: 'In philosophy I can only recommend the Three "A"s', she would often say: 'Aristotle, Aquinas and Ayn Rand!' The move towards reason is clearly not the most distinctive aspect of Rand's philosophy, though it may be the most interesting – and appealing.

In fact, the true break with previous writing in this Stirnerian and Modernist tradition is a consequence of her refusal to question a key premise underpinning the subjectivist rebellion against utopia; her originality within the new context that has been established in this essay is the direct result of an unquestioning acceptance of the assumption that *whim* is a characteristic of the subconscious. 'To the irrationalist', Nathaniel Branden explains, 'existence is merely a clash between *his* whims and the whims of *others*; the concept of an *objective* reality has no reality for him'.[73] The consequences that must result from this attempt to amputate *whim*, the desire for an 'independence from reality', are spelled out by Rand's contemporary, the anarchist Murray Rothbard in a letter to his friend Richard Cornuelle, written in 1954, when he claims: 'she actually denies all individuality whatsoever!' His reason for saying so would have provoked nothing but scorn from Rand, for he is clearly adopting the subjectivist or irrationalist position when he states that individuality consists in emotions and in instinct. But this in no way invalidates his point: to assert men are 'bundles of premises', in the way that Rand does, before proceeding to outline *what* the premises *ought* to be for *a man of reason*, is to effect a negation of the individual self – because the individual self is thereby rendered interchangeable with any other individual self – only provided the latter is sufficiently rational enough. 'There is no reason [therefore] whatsoever, why Ayn, for example, shouldn't sleep with Nathan', Rothbard concludes.[74] The faculty of reason has been set up above and beyond the self – in a totalizing system that must refuse to accept as fully human anyone that refuses to conform to what is deemed reason. The rational self is rendered impervious to any further *analysis* (ἀναλύω: 'I unravel') – Stirner's perpetual negation of the posited *persona*. This is the point whereon Rand differs most from earlier writers in the Stirnerian tradition. Not on reason *per se* – but on whether being a *man of reason* is compatible with your believing that you might change your mind to suit yourself – on whether you have the right to assert your independence from objective reality through continuous mercurial acts of self-renewal.

In fact, over the course of her long life Rand was, of course, capable of the most breathtaking feats of self-reinvention (not least when a young Russian called Alyssa Rosenbaum transformed herself into the American Rand), disorientating those around her with sudden, unacknowledged reorganizations of her personal history. That Rand possessed this capacity for *ecstasy* or *ek-stasis*, for *standing forth* from her given situation, is only surprising if one accepts her Objectivist philosophy. In fact, 'it is our very incapacity ... to constitute ourselves as being what we are', remarks Sartre, 'which means that, as soon as we posit ourselves as a certain being, by a legitimate judgment, based on an inner experience or correctly deduced from *a priori* or empirical premises, then by that very positing we surpass this being – and that not toward another being but toward emptiness, toward *nothing*'.[75] The point we lose this *nothing* that separates *us* from *what we are* is the very moment of death. No longer is there this *nothing* between our selves and our past: we become our past, forever fixed, an empirical fact. But like Marx and Engels, a century earlier, Rand would eventually condemn this Stirnerian '*Reification of the Zero*' as mere 'juggling tricks on the tight-rope of the objective'.[76]

It consists of regarding "nothing" as a *thing*, as a special, different kind of *existent*. (For example, see Existentialism.) This fallacy breeds such symptoms as the notion that presence and absence, or being and non-being, are metaphysical forces of equal power, and that being is the absence of non-being. E.g., "Nothingness is prior to being". (Sartre) – "Human finitude is the presence of the not in the being of man". (William Barrett) – "Nothing is more real than nothing". (Samuel Beckett) – "*Das Nichts nichtet*" or "Nothing noughts." (Heidegger). "Consciousness, then, is not a stuff, but a *negation*. The subject is not a thing, but a *non-thing*. The subject carves its own world out of Being by means of negative determinations. Sartre describes consciousness as a 'noughting nought' (*néant néantisant*). It is a form of being other than its own: a mode 'which has yet to be what it is, that is to say, which is what it is, that is to say, which is what it is not and which is not what it was.'"[77]

However, even Rand could not sustain an existence that could proceed as though such 'concept-stealing' were not inevitable – live in a way that might vindicate her identification of the rational subject with his/her objective reality. In calling for this equation to take place, Rand condemned herself, and her disciples, to Bad Faith.

Curiously, Rand once toyed with calling her philosophy *Existentialism* (until told the name was taken). Chosen to reflect a definitive break with subjectivism, her refusal of solipsism, Rand's turn towards *Objectivism* perfectly describes what her system became. Where Stirner had pre-empted the Existentialists in asserting that the ego possessed a continual capacity for ecstatic disavowal, Rand's Subject must try to live as though one with its conception of a rational self, to live being its own object. If the consequences are not sufficiently clear, read Nathaniel Branden's harrowing account of trying to break off a *perfectly logical* affair with Rand. If this peculiar brand of egoism does continue to work as a defence against the depredations of external authority, it can no longer do anything to protect the individual from forms of self-oppression, tyrannies far worse than anything that might have been imposed from outside because all-pervasive, internalized. Where Stirner resolved to become his own cause and to set this cause upon nothing, Rand relinquished the capacity for self-analysis that alone guaranteed the freedom of the ego – and thereby lapsed from egoism into chauvinism, that is to say, the subordination of the self to a cause that appears to require no sacrifice (as in altruism) because the cause is ones own, but where the ego is no less a slave to a cause for all that – the cause being one's persona, one's own status as an object. In short: *Objectivism* is not a philosophy for living but rather for those who would be living dead.

Consequences

In 'The Lesbian Session', his famous essay on Rand in *Lacanian Ink,* Slavoj Žižek has observed that 'although it is easy to dismiss the very mention of Rand in a "serious" theoretical article as an obscene extravaganza – artistically, she is of course, worthless – the properly subversive dimension of her ideological procedure is not to be underestimated'.[78] In fact, Žižek then goes on to suggest, 'Rand fits into the line of over-conformist authors who undermine the ruling ideological edifice by their very excessive identification with it'.[79] Having traced the development of Rand's ideas in considerable detail, we are now in a position to establish the precise nature, and extent, of this properly subversive dimension.

Developed in one of the three most oppressive autocracies of nineteenth-century Europe, Stirnerian egoism was designed to effect wholesale destruction, to poison any political system into which it was introduced, to render the altruist morality required to sustain collective enterprise impossible through perpetual insurrection or general strike, a withdrawal of properties and powers on the part of those resolved to put no cause before their own freedom for creative negation. Rand's philosophy, though differing in certain respects, is at one with the original in its political intent. No one who reads *Atlas Shrugged* can be under any illusion on this point. Rand is clear on the consequences that must follow for the United States if only a sufficient number of Americans began to participate in a political insurrection of the sort she imagines. John Galt really does stop the motor of the world.

Yet every day brings new stories of insurrection on the part of those rich and powerful no longer prepared to sacrifice themselves to a political system based on altruism. As Žižek has remarked, in a caustic op-ed for *The Guardian*, we now know precisely who John Galt is: 'John Galt is the idiot responsible for the 2008 financial meltdown, and for the ongoing federal government shut down in the US.'[80] Having persuaded her readers that 'Big Business' is 'America's most persecuted minority', Rand prevents any further act of self-appraisal that might prevent such selfishness from ossifying into a pursuit of fixed ideas that eventually begin to work against their own self-interest. Having bought the Rand line on insurrection, these readers are 'locked into the product' right to the end. Let us be quite clear on this point. If the Union of States established by the American Revolution collapses this will be because those with the most to lose from such a scenario have consciously adopted and consistently promoted a radical Hegelian philosophy that is fundamentally hostile to the Lockean political principles that underpin the system upon which they depend. (A fact not often noted in relation to Rand's last novel: even millionaires living in a 'Utopia of Greed' are compelled, having effected the collapse of civilization, to muck out their own pigs by hand.) Might the unrelenting insurrection of the Super-Rich actually constitute the most monstrous self-abnegation? This is your wakeup call. Good morning, America!

NOTES

Preface

1   Drew Goddard in conversation with *Filmmaker Magazine* (10 April 2012).
Available at http://filmmakermagazine.com/43750-a-conversation-with-cabin-in-thewoods-director-drew-goddard/#.VafkZotiHx4

2   See Frederic Jameson, *Postmodernism, or, The Cultural Logic of Late Capitalism* (London: Verso, 1991).

3   Ayn Rand, 'The Objectivist Ethics' [1961]. *The Virtue of Selfishness* (New York: Signet, 1964), 34.

4   Ibid., 30.

5   Ibid., 29.

6   Ibid., 27.

7   Auberon Herbert to Mr Radnor, *The Free Life*, July 1898.

8   Ibid.

9   This point is put to John Galt, the man behind the Strike, by one Dr Ferris, who notes that there are also 'sins of omission'… But he botches his case by suggesting, 'it might become necessary to issue a directive ordering that every third one of all children under ten and all adults over the age of sixty be put to death, to secure the survival of the rest' … and that all these executions would be John Galt's fault and his moral responsibility. As Galt points out, *his* moral stature is not to be determined by the government's reactions. But the larger point relating to the millions of deaths resulting from the famine caused by the Strike is permitted to go unchallenged. And the egoist role in this catastrophe is not entirely passive. Francisco d'Anconia and Ragnar Danneskjöld both engage in sabotage to hasten the end of the system. Francisco lures investors into sinking a considerable portion of the country's wealth into a mine that he knows to be 'blatantly, totally, hopelessly worthless', while Danneskjöld is a pirate who preys upon US aid-shipments, in order to restore the wealth to *America's most persecuted minority*. In his own words, '[Robin Hood] was the man who

robbed the rich and gave to the poor. Well, I'm the man who robs the poor and gives to the rich – or, to be exact, the man who robs the thieving poor and gives back to the productive rich...' See Ayn Rand, *Atlas Shrugged* (London: Penguin, 2007), 53, 89, 576.

10   Ibid., 1158.

11   Ibid., 1168.

12   See Chris Matthew Sciabarra, *Ayn Rand: The Russian Radical* (Pennsylvania State University Press, 1995), 67.

13   Nathaniel Branden, 'Counterfeit Individualism', Ayn Rand, *The Virtue of Selfishness: A New Concept of Egoism*, 158.

14   Gerald F. Gaus and Fred D'Agostino, *Routledge Companion to Social and Political Philosophy* (London: Routledge, 2013), 221.

15   Robert Graham, *Anarchism: From Anarchy to Anarchism (300CE–1939), Vol. 1: A Documentary History of Libertarian Ideas* (Montreal: Black Rose Books, 2005), xiii.

16   'The most disheartening tendency common among readers is to tear out one sentence from a work, as a criterion of the writer's ideas or personality... It is the same narrow attitude which sees in Max Stirner naught but the apostle of the theory "each for himself, the devil take the hind one." That Stirner's individualism contains the greatest social possibilities is utterly ignored. Yet, it is nevertheless true that if society is ever to become free, it will be so through liberated individuals, whose free efforts make society'. –Emma Goldman, *Anarchism and Other Essays* (New York: Mother Earth Publishing Association, 1910), 50.

17   'Here we can feel the somber joy of those who create an apocalypse in a garret. This bitter and imperious logic can no longer be held in check, except by an I which is determined to defeat every form of abstraction and which has itself become abstract and nameless through being isolated and cut off from its roots.... Since every I is, in itself, fundamentally criminal in its attitude toward the State and the people, we must recognise that to live is to transgress. Unless we accept death, we must be willing to kill in order to be unique... But to decree that murder is legitimate is to decree mobilisation and war for all the Unique. Thus murder will coincide with a kind of collective suicide'. –Albert Camus, *The Rebel* [1951]. Trans. Anthony Bower (New York: Random House, 1956), 62–65. For Herbert Read's perspective see, for instance, the chapter on Stirner in *The Tenth Muse* (London: Routledge and Kegan Paul, 1957).

18 'The long revolution is preparing to write works in the ink of action, works whose unknown or nameless authors will flock to join de Sade, Fourier, Babeuf, Marx, Lacenaire, Stirner, Lautréamont, Léhautier, Vaillant, Henry, Villa, Makhno, the Communards, the insurrectionaries of Hamburg, Kiel, Kronstadt, Asturias – all those who have not yet played their last card in a game which we have only just joined, the great gamble whose stake is freedom'. –Raoul Veneigem, *The Revolution of Everyday Life* [1967]. Trans. David Nicholson-Smith (London: Rebel Press, 2006), 63.

19 'Egoism in its narrowest sense is a tautology, not a tactic. Adolescents of all ages who triumphantly trumpet that "everyone is selfish," as if they'd made a factual discovery about the world, only show that they literally don't know what they're talking about. Practical egoism must be something more, it must tell the egoist something useful about himself and other selves which will make a difference in his life (and, as it happens, theirs). My want, needs, desires, whims – call them what you will – extend the ego, which is my-self purposively acting, out where the other selves await me. If I deal with them, as the economists say, "at arm's length," I can't get as close as I need to for so much of what I want. At any rate, no "spook," no ideology is going to get in my way. Do you have ideas, or do ideas have you?' –From Bob Black's 'Preface to the Preface'. For Ourselves: The Council for Generalized Self-Management, *The Right to be Greedy: Theses on the Practical Necessity of Demanding Everything* [1974], ed. B. Black (Port Townsend, WA: Loompanics Unlimited, 1983).

20 'Human or divine, as Stirner said, the predicates are the same whether they belong analytically to the divine being, or whether they are synthetically bound to the human form'. – Gilles Deleuze, *The Logic of Sense* [1969]. Trans. Mark Lester. Ed. Constantin V. Boundas (London and New York: Continuum, 2004), 122.

21 'As will be spelled out later on the basis of *The German Ideology* and the argument with Stirner, what distinguishes the specter or the *revenant* from the *spirit*, including the spirit in the sense of the ghost in general, is doubtless a supernatural and paradoxical phenomenality, the furtive and ungraspable visibility of the invisible, or an invisibility of a visible X, that *non-sensuous sensuous* of which *Capital* speaks (we will come to this) with regard to a certain exchange-value...' –Jacques Derrida, *Specters of Marx* [1993]. Trans. Peggy Kamuf (New York and London: Routledge, 2006), 6.

22 Gaus and D'Agostino, *Routledge Companion to Social and Political Philosophy*, 221.

23 Nathaniel Branden, 'Counterfeit Individualism', 158.

24 T.S. Eliot, 'Tradition and the Individual Talent' [1917]. *The Sacred Wood* (London: Methuen and Co., 1920, 1960), 56.

25 'If [Stanley Coffman] reads the movement as anti-individualist, it is no doubt because the movement would go on to read itself that way. I have been trying to show at some length the inadequacy of that reading, to point out that modernism was individualist before it was anti-individualist, anti-traditional before it was traditional, inclined to anarchism before it was inclined to authoritarianism'. –Michael H. Levenson, *A Genealogy of Modernism* (Cambridge University Press, 1984), 79.

Chapter 1

1 Richard Huelsenbeck, *En Avant Dada: A History of Dadaism* [1920]. Trans. Ralph Manheim. Reproduced in *The Dada Painters and Poets: An Anthology*, ed. Robert Motherwell (Cambridge, MA and London: Harvard University Press, 1951/1981), 32.

2 Ibid., 41.

3 Ibid., 33.

4 Ibid., 37.

5 Theresa Papanikolas, *Anarchism and the Advent of Paris Dada: Art and Criticism 1914–1924* (Farnham, Surrey: Ashgate, 2010), 1.

6 See Michel Sanouillet, *Dada à Paris* [1965], English language edition: trans. Sharmila Ganguly (MIT Press, 2012); William Rubin, *Dada and Surrealist Art* (New York: Henry N. Adams, 1969).

7 Sanouillet, 429–430.

8 Papanikolas, 1.

9 Ibid., 4–5.

10 Tristan Tzara, *Dada Manifesto* 1918. Trans. Ralph Manheim. *The Dada Painters and Poets*, 81.

11 Papanikolas, 5.

12 Ibid., 10.

13 Huelsenbeck, 30.

14   James Huneker, *Egoists: A Book of Supermen* (New York: C. Scribner's Sons, 1921), 351–352.

15   John F. Welsh, *Max Stirner's Dialectical Egoism: A New Interpretation* (New York: Lexington Books, 2010), 3.

16   Edgar Bauer to Max Hildebrandt, 1882: Available online at: www. nonserviam.com/egoistarchive/stirner/articles/Step_StirnerAndSeliga2. htm

17   Huneker, 350.

18   Max Stirner, *The Ego and His Own: The Case of the Individual against Authority* [1844]. Translated by Steven T. Byington [1907]. Ed. James L. Martin [1963]. Facsimile reprint (New York: Dover, 2005), 4.

19   Ibid., 9.

20   Ibid., 10.

21   Ibid., 11.

22   Ibid., 13.

23   Ibid., 14.

24   Ibid., 67.

25   Ibid., 32.

26   Ibid., 33.

27   Ibid., 127.

28   Ibid., 37.

29   Ibid., 116.

30   Ibid., 43.

31   Ibid., 167.

32   Ibid., 166.

33   Ibid., 157.

34   Ibid., 316.

35   Ibid., 179.

36   Ibid., 316.

37   Ibid., 357.

38 Ibid., 182.

39 Ibid., 339

40 Ibid., 361.

41 Ibid., 182.

42 Ibid., 150.

43 The literal translation of Stirner's final lines: 'Stell' Ich auf Mich meine Sache … Ich hab' Mein' Sach' auf Nichts gestellt.' Byington paraphrases this as: 'If I concern myself for myself, the unique one, then my concern rests on its transitory, mortal creator, who consumes himself, and I may say: … All things are nothing to me'. (Stirner, p. 366.) The English cognate for German 'Sache' is near extinct, but still familiar: 'my sake' ought to convey the sense of an expression for which there is no longer an easy equivalent in English.

44 Karl Marx and Friedrich Engels, *The German Ideology* [1845–1847]: *Collected Works* Vol. 5. Translated by Clemens Dutt, W. Lough, C.P. Magill (London: Lawrence and Wishart, 1976), 120.

45 Ibid., 129.

46 Ibid., 229.

47 Ibid., 130.

48 Ibid., 241.

49 Ibid., 266.

50 Ibid.

51 Welsh, 21.

52 Herbert Read, *The Tenth Muse* (London: Routledge and Kegan Paul, 1957), 75.

53 Karl Marx, *A Contribution to the Critique of Political Economy* [1859], *Collected Works* Vol. 29 (London: Lawrence and Wishart, 1971), 22.

54 Marx and Engels, *The German Ideology*, 293.

55 Engels, Letter to Marx, 19 November 1844. See "Correspondence", Marx and Engels Collected Works, Vol. 38 (London: Lawrence and Wishart, 1982), 12.

56 Richard Parry, *The Bonnot Gang: The Story of the French Illegalists* (London: Rebel Press, 1987), 28.

57 The Bonnot Gang appear to invented the concept of the getaway car. According to Parry, the first drive-by hold-up in the US, reported in the *London Times*, took place on 23 September 1912, nearly nine months after 'the rue Ordener Outrage'. *Les bandits en auto* were generally considered to be entirely 'without precedent in the history of crime'. See Parry, 83.

58 Parry, 85.

59 Garnier, Letter to the Police, *Le Matin*, 21 March 1912, trans. Parry, 111.

60 Ibid., 135, 138.

61 Garnier, 'My Memoirs' [1912]; trans. Parry, 146.

62 Parry, 166.

63 René Hemme (Mauricius), *L'Anarchie* (17 April 1913), cited Jean Maitron, *Le Mouvement anarchiste en France* (Paris: François Maspero, 1975), 435, n. 75.

64 Parry, 167.

65 Ibid.

66 Ibid., 171.

67 Ibid. 172.

68 Papanikolas, 40.

69 Ibid., 41.

70 Florent Fels, 'Une Littérature d'avant-garde; l'esprit nouveau', *La Mêlée* (1 November 1919), 1.

71 For further detail on *Action* (1920–1922) and its contributors see Papanikolas, 46–47.

72 Tzara, 78.

73 Papanikolas, 88–89.

74 Hugo Ball, diary entry 23 June 1915, *Flight Out of Time: A Dada Diary*, ed. John Elderfield (Berkeley: University of California Press, 1996), 71.

75 Tzara, 78.

76 Georges Ribemont-Dessaignes, 'Ce qu'il faut pas dire sur l'art', *La Vie des Lettres 7* (January 1921), reprinted in Georges Ribemont-Dessaignes, *Manifestes Dada: Poèms, Articles Projets, 1915–1920*, ed. Jean-Pierre Begot (Paris: Editions Champ Libre, 1974), 25.

77 Louis Aragon, 'Manifesto of the Dada Movement', *Litterature* 13 (1920), 1.

78 Huelsenbeck, 33.

79 Ibid., 36.

80 Allan Antliff, *Anarchy and Art: From the Paris Commune to the Fall of the Berlin Wall* (Vancouver, BC: Arsenal Pulp Press, 2007), 49.

81 Francis Picabia, 'A Post-Cubist's Impressions of New York', *New York Tribune* (9 March 1913). Quoted by Antliff, 53.

82 See Papanikolas, 1–7.

83 Fransis Picabia, 'Manifeste Cannibale Dada' [March 1920], *Écrits critiques* (Paris: Mémoire du livre, 2005), 213.

84 Antliff, 53.

85 Papanikolas, 102.

86 Huelsenbeck, 37.

87 Tristan Tzara, 'Manifesto of Feeble Love and Bitter Love', *The Dada Painters and Poets*, 92.

88 Duchamp in interview: *Marcel Duchamp: Works, Writing and Interviews*, ed. Gloria Moure (Barcelona: Ediciones Polígrafa, 1984), 232.

89 Ibid., 232.

90 Francis M. Naumann, 'Marcel Duchamp: A Reconciliation of Opposites', *The Definitively Unfinished Marcel Duchamp*, ed. Thierry de Duve (Cambridge, MA: MIT Press, 1991), 53.

91 Craig Adcock in conversation with Francis M. Naumann, *The Definitively Unfinished Marcel Duchamp*, 67.

92 Marcel Duchamp, 'The 1914 Box', *The Writings of Marcel Duchamp*, eds. Michel Sanouillet and Elmer Peterson (New York: De Capo Press, 1973), 22.

93 Ibid., 22.

94 Ibid.

95 Duchamp, as quoted in *Marcel Duchamp*, eds. Anne d'Harnoncourt and Kynaston L. McShine (New York: Museum of Modern Art, 1984), 273–274.

96 Naumann, 54.

97 Ibid.

98 Duchamp, 'The 1914 Box', 22.

99 R.S. Longhurst, *Geometrical and Physical Optics* (Longmans: London, 1968).

100 P. Hariharan, *Basics of Interferometry* (Amsterdam: Elsevier, 2007), 17.

101 Duchamp, 'The Great Trouble with Art in this Country' (1946), *The Writings of Marcel Duchamp*, 125.

102 Ibid.

103 Duchamp, 'Apropos of "Readymades" [1961]', *The Writings of Marcel Duchamp*, 141.

104 Ibid.

105 See Stirner, 91–93.

106 Duchamp, 'The Creative Act' [1957], *The Writings of Marcel Duchamp*, 138, 140.

107 Ibid., 139.

108 Ibid.

109 Ibid., 140.

110 G.W.F. Hegel, *Lectures on the Philosophy of Religion* [1832], ed. Peter C. Hodgson (Oxford: Oxford University Press, 2006), 298.

111 G.W.F. Hegel, *Lectures on the Philosophy of History* [1847]. Translated by J Sibree. Ed. CJ Friedrich (New York: Dover, 1956), 93–94.

112 Hegel, *Philosophy of Religion*, 309.

113 Hegel, *Philosophy of History*, 94.

114 Stirner, 339.

115 Ibid., 335.

116 Ibid., 333.

117 Ibid., 339.

118 Karl Marx, *Capital: A Critique of Political Economy, Vol. One*. Translated by Ben Fowkes (London: Penguin, 1976), 163.

119 Ibid.

120 Ibid., 165.

121 Ibid., 163.

122 Ibid., 165.

123   Ibid., 167.

124   Ibid.

125   Ibid.

126   Karl Menger, *Principles of Economics*. Translated by James Dingwall and Bert F. Hoselitz (Sussex: Terre Libertas, 1976), 116, 146.

127   Engels, Letter to Marx, 19 November 1844. Available online at: www. marxists.org

128   Karl Menger, *Principles of Economics*. Translated by James Dingwall and Bert F. Hoselitz (Terra Libertas: Eastbourne, Sussex, 2011), 141, 147.

129   Damien Hirst cited in Damien Hirst and Gordon Burn, 'On the Way to Work' (Faber and Faber: London, 2001), 162.

130   Grayson Perry, 'Playing to the Gallery – Democracy Has Bad Taste', Reith Lectures 2013. Delivered at the Tate Modern and broadcast on Radio 4. Transcript available at: http://downloads.bbc.co.uk/radio4/transcripts/lecture-1-transcript.pdf

131   Will Self, 'Are the Hyper-Rich Ruining the New Tate Modern?', *The Guardian*, 21 November 2014. Available online at: http://www.theguardian.com/artanddesign/2014/nov/21/will-self-are-the-hyper-rich-ruining-the-new-tate-modern

132   André Breton, *Conversations: The Autobiography of Surrealism*. Translated by Mark Polizzotti (Boston: Marlowe and Co., 1995), 53.

133   Tristan Tzara, 'Les Témoins: Tristan Tzara', *Littérature* 20 (1921): 10–11.

134   Breton, 'Characteristics of the Modern Evolution and What It Consists Of', in *The Lost Steps*. Translated by Mark Polizotti (Lincoln: University of Nebraska Press, 1996), 123.

Chapter 2

1   T.S. Eliot, 'Preface to Edition of 1964', *The Use of Poetry and the Use of Criticism* [1933] (London: Faber and Faber, 1964), 9–10.

2   T.S. Eliot, 'Tradition and the Individual Talent' [1917], *The Sacred Wood* (London: Methuen and Co., 1920, 1960), 53.

3   Ibid., 56.

4   Eliot, 'Egoists, by James Huneker', *Harvard Advocate* 88:1, 5 October
     1909; 16.

5   Pound et al., 'Views and Comments', *The New Freewoman*,
     15 December 1913; 244.

6   John. F. Welsh, *Max Stirner's Dialectical Egoism: A New Interpretation*
     (New York: Lexington Books, 2010), 222.

7   Ibid., 223.

8   See Michael H. Levenson, *A Genealogy of Modernism* (Cambridge:
     Cambridge University Press, 1984), 79.

9   Friedrich Nietzsche, Letter to his Mother, 22 October 1865. Translated by
     Bernd A. Laska. 'Nietsche's Initial Crisis' – *Germanic Notes & Reviews*, 33:2
     (Herbst, 2002), 109–133.

10   Carl Albrecht Bernoulli: *Franz Overbeck und Friedrich Nietzsche – eine
     Freundschaft*. 2 Bände. (Jena: Eugen Diederichs, 1908), 238.

11   Franz Overbeck, *Erinnerungen an Friedrich Nietzsche* (Neue Rundschau,
     February 1906), 209–231.

12   Eduard von Hartmann: 'Nietzsches "neue Moral"', *Preussische Jahrbücher*,
     67:5, May 1891; 501–521.

13   Dora Marsden, 'Views and Comments', *The New Freewoman*, 1:13,
     15 December 1913; 244.

14   Marsden, 'Bondwomen', *The Freewoman*, I:1, 23 November 1911; 1

15   Marsden, 'The Growing Ego', *The Freewoman*, II:38, 8 August 1912; 222

16   Marsden, 'Concerning the Beautiful', *The New Freewoman*, I:6, 1 September
     1913; 104.

17   Marsden, 'Skyscapes and Goodwill', *The Egoist*, II:1, 15 January 1914; 24.

18   Marsden, 'The Lean Kind', *The New Freewoman*, I:1, 15 June 1913; 4.

19   Marsden, 'I Am', *The Egoist*, II:1, 1 January 1915; 1.

20   Marsden, 'The Lean Kind', *The New Freewoman*, I:1, 15 June 1913; 5.

21   Ibid.

22   Marsden, 'The Heart of the Question', *The New Freewoman*, I:4,
     1 August 1913; 65.

23 Ibid.

24 Marsden, 'Views and Comments', *The New Freewoman*, I:13,
    15 December 1913; 245.

25 Ibid., 244.

26 Letter to the Editor, *The New Freewoman*, I:2, 15 November 1913; 204.

27 Marsden, 'Views and Comments', *The Egoist*, I:5, 2 March 1914; 84–85.

28 Marsden, 'The Illusion of Anarchism', *The Egoist*, I:18,
    15 September 1914; 342.

29 Ibid.

30 Ibid.

31 Marsden, 'Views and Comments', *The Egoist*, I:5, 2 March 1914; 84.

32 Marsden, 'The Illusion of Anarchism', *The Egoist*, I:18,
    15 September 1914; 314.

33 Welsh, 221–222.

34 Ibid.

35 Rachel Blau Du-Plessis, *Pink Guitar: Writing as Feminist Practice*
    (Tuscaloosa: University of Alabama Press, 2006), 45.

36 Ibid., 45.

37 Bruce Clarke, *Dora Marsden and Early Modernism: Gender, Individualism,
    Science* (Michigan: University of Michigan Press, 1996), 9.

38 Marsden, 'Some Critics Answered', *The Egoist*, II:2, 1 February 1915; 17.

39 Marsden, 'I Am', *The Egoist*, II:1, January 1915; 2.

40 Ibid., 2–3.

41 Marsden, 'Lingual Psychology: A New Conception of the Function of
    Philosophic Inquiry', *The Egoist*, III:7, July 1916, 97.

42 Ibid.

43 Marsden, 'The Art of the Future', *The New Freewoman*, I:10, 1 November
    1913; 183.

44 Marsden, 'Views and Comments', *The New Freewoman*, I:18, 15 December
    1913; 245.

45 Ibid., I:9, 15 October 1913; 163.

46 Clarke, 102.

47 Marsden, 'I Am', *The Egoist*, II:1, 1 January 1915; 4.

48 F.H. Bradley, *Appearance and Reality: A Metaphysical Essay* (Oxford: Clarendon Press, 1893, 1930), 346.

49 Marsden, 'The Science of Signs XVII. Truth IV. The Measure of Authority which Egoism allows to the Science of External Nature', *The Egoist*, VI:3, July 1919; 34; "The Science of Signs XVII. Truth V. How the Theory of the Ego requires us to Construe Death", *The Egoist*, VI:4, September 1919; 50.

50 Marsden, 'I Am', *The Egoist*, II:1, 1 January 1915; 4.

51 Ibid.

52 Ibid.

53 Ibid.

54 Marsden, 'Truth and Reality', *The Egoist*, II:4, 1 April 1915; 51.

55 Marsden, 'I Am', *The Egoist*, II:1, January 1915; 4.

56 Marsden, 'The Science of Signs XVII. Truth II. The Processes Involved in Its Growth', *The Egoist*, VI:1, January–February 1919; 2.

57 Marsden, 'Lingual Psychology VIII: Language and the Origination of the Concept', *The Egoist*, IV:4, May 1917; 49.

58 Marsden, 'The Constitution and Origin of the "Image" in the Imagination', *The Egoist*, IV:3, April 1917; 46.

59 Ibid.

60 Marsden, 'The Science of Signs XVII. Truth III. The Meaning of Error', *The Egoist*, VI:2, March–April 1919; 20.

61 Ibid.

62 Ibid.

63 Marsden, 'Lingual Psychology IX. Notes on the Origin of Conceptual Activity', *The Egoist*, IV:5, July 1917; 82.

64 Ibid.

65 Marsden, 'The Science of Signs XVIII: The Egoistic Interpretation of Future Time', *The Egoist*, VI:5, December 1919; 70.

66 Ibid., 67.

67 Ibid., 70.

68 Marsden, 'Truth and Reality', *The Egoist*, II:4, April 1915; 53.

69 Marsden, 'The Art of the Future', *The New Freewoman*, I:10,
    1 November 1913; 182.

70 Ibid.

71 Marsden, 'Intellect and Culture', *The New Freewoman*, I:2, 1 July 1913; 22.

72 Marsden, 'The Art of the Future', *The New Freewoman*, I:10,
    1 November 1913; 182.

73 Marsden, 'I Am', *The Egoist*, II:1, 1 January 1915; 2.

74 Marsden, 'Truth and Reality', *The Egoist*, II:4, 1 April 1915; 50.

75 Ibid., 53.

76 Glenn Hughes, *Imagism and the Imagists: A Study in Modern Poetry*
    (New York: Biblo and Tannen, 1960), 31–32.

77 Ibid.

78 Welsh, 223.

79 Ibid.

80 Letter from Marsden to Harriet Shaw Weaver, October 1915. Quoted Leslie
    Garner, *A Brave and Beautiful Spirit: Dora Marsden, 1882–1960* (Aldershot:
    Avebury, 1990), 136.

81 A. David Moody, *Ezra Pound: Poet, Vol. I: The Young Genius 1885–1920*
    (Oxford: Oxford University Press, 2007), 222.

82 Ibid., 221.

83 Ibid.

84 Ezra Pound, 'The Serious Artist', *The New Freewoman*, I:9, 15 October
    1913; 161.

85 Marsden, 'Skyscapes and Goodwill', *The Egoist*, I:2, 15 January 1915; 2.

86 Ezra Pound, 'A Few Don'ts by an Imagiste', *Poetry: A Magazine of Verse*
    (Chicago, March 1913) Vol. 1, No. 6; 201.

87 William Carlos Williams, *Paterson* (New York: New Directions, 1995), 6.

88 Marsden, 'I Am', *The Egoists*, II:1, 1 January 1915; 3.

89 Marsden, 'Intellect and Culture', *The New Freewoman*, I:2, 1 July 1913; 23.

90   Pound, 'A Few Don'ts …', 204.

91   Pound, 'The Wisdom of Poetry', *Forum* (New York, April 1912), 332.

92   Ibid.

93   Pound, *The Fortnightly Review*, September 1914; 467.

94   Marsden, 'The Art of the Future', *The New Freewoman*, I:10, 1 November 1913; 182.

95   Ibid.

96   Ibid., 183.

97   Ibid.

98   Ibid.

99   Ibid.

100 Ibid.

101 Pound, *The Fortnightly Review*, September 1914; 463–464.

102 Pound, 'As for Imagisme', *The New Age*, XVI, 28 January 1915; 349.

103 Pound, 'Vortex', *BLAST 1*, 1914; 153.

104 Williams Carlos Williams, *Spring and All* [1923], ed. C.D. Wright (New York: New Directions, 2011), 14.

105 T.S. Eliot, *Knowledge and Experience: In the Philosophy of FH Bradley* (New York: Farrar, Strauss and Company, 1964), 166.

106 Ibid., 91.

107 Ibid., 148–149.

108 Ibid., 206.

109 Ibid., 202.

110 Ibid., 163.

111 Eliot, 'East Coker: II', [1940], 'Dry Salvages: III' [1941], *Collected Poems 1909–1962* (London: Faber and Faber, 1963), 199.

112 Eliot, *Knowledge and Experience*, 148–149.

113 Marsden, 'The Science of Signs XVII. Truth V. How the Theory of the Ego Requires Us to Construe Death', *The Egoist*, VI:4, September 1919; 52.

114 Ibid.

115   Ibid.

116   Eliot, 'Coriolan I: Triumphal March' [1930], *Collected Poems*, 139.
       Edmund Husserl, *Ideas: General Introduction to Pure Phenomenology*
       [1913]. Translated by W.R. Boyce Gibson [1931]. Ed. Dermot Moran
       (London and New York: Routledge, 2012), II:39; 74.

117   Clarke, 102.

118   Dora Marsden, *The Mysteries of Christianity* (London: Egoist Press,
       1930), 256.

119   Marsden, *The New Freewoman*, 15 November 1913; 202.

Chapter 3

1   Wyndham Lewis, 'Enemy of the Stars', *BLAST 1*, ed. Michel Sanouillet
       (Santa Rosa: Black Sparrow Press, 2002), 76–77.

2   Paul Edwards, *Wyndham Lewis: Painter and Writer* (New Haven: Yale
       University Press, 2000), 157.

3   Lewis, 'Enemy of the Stars', 77.

4   Ibid., 74, 64.

5   Edwards, 156.

6   Lewis, 'Enemy of the Stars', 77.

7   Ibid.

8   Edwards, 555.

9   Lewis, *BLAST 1*, 67.

10   Ibid., 59.

11   Ibid., 65.

12   Ibid., 59.

13   Wyndham Lewis, *The Art of Being Ruled* [1926], ed. Reed Way
       Dasenbrock (Santa Rosa: Black Sparrow Press, 1989), 255.

14   Ibid., 257.

15   Ibid.

16   Lewis, *BLAST 1*, 25.

17   Wyndham Lewis, *The Caliph's Design* [1919], ed. Paul Edwards (Santa Rosa: Black Sparrow Press, 1986), 66.

18   Lewis, *The Art of Being Ruled*, 267.

19   Wyndham Lewis, *Time and Western Man* [1928], ed. Paul Edwards (Santa Rosa: Black Sparrow Press, 1993), 187.

20   Ibid.,188.

21   Lewis, *The Art of Being Ruled*, 267.

22   Lewis, *BLAST 1*, 33.

23   Ibid., 146.

24   Max Stirner, *The Ego and His Own* [1844]. Translated by Steven T. Byington [1907]. Ed. James J. Martin (New York: Dover, 2005), 71.

25   Lewis, *BLAST 1*, 61; Stirner, 70.

26   Lewis, *BLAST 1*, 59, 55.

27   Edwards, 158.

28   Wyndham Lewis, 'The Ideal Giant' [1917]. *Collected Poems and Plays*, ed. Alan Munton (Manchester: Carcenet, 1996), 131.

29   Lewis, *BLAST 1*, 66.

30   Ibid., 71.

31   Ibid., 70.

32   Ibid., 68.

33   Ibid., 141.

34   Ibid., 84.

35   Ibid., 61.

36   Edwards, 158.

37   Ibid., 144.

38   Ibid.

39   Ibid.

40   Lewis, *BLAST 1*, 67–68.

41   Wyndham Lewis, 'Inferior Religions', *The Wild Body* (London: Chatto and Windus, 1927), 235.

42   Ibid., 238.

43   Wyndham Lewis, 'The Meaning of the Wild Body', *The Wild Body* (London: Chatto and Windus, 1927), 243.

44   Lewis, 'Inferior Religions', 236.

45   Ibid., 236.

46   Wyndham Lewis, *The Childermass* (London: Jupiter Books, 1965), 149.

47   Ibid.

48   R.D. Laing, *The Divided Self* (London: Penguin 1990), 22.

49   Lewis, *BLAST 1*, 66.

50   Lewis, 'Inferior Religions', 236.

51   Wyndham Lewis, 'Imaginary Letters: Letter III', *The Little Review* 4:11, (March 1918); 23–30, 24.

52   Lewis, *Time and Western Man*, 377.

53   Ibid., 372.

54   Ibid., 377.

55   Ibid., 372.

56   Ibid., 376.

57   Ibid., 370.

58   Wyndham, Lewis, *The Apes of God* [1930], ed. Paul Edwards (Santa Rosa: Black Sparrow Press, 1997), 118.

59   Ibid., 125.

60   Ibid., 291.

61   Edwards, 351.

62   Lewis, *The Childermass*, 394.

63   Edwards, 351.

64   Wyndham Lewis, *Rude Assignment* [1950], ed. Toby Foshay (Santa Rosa: Black Sparrow Press, 1984), 183.

65 Wyndham Lewis, *Tarr* (London: Chatto and Windus, 1928), 303.

66 Lewis, *Time and Western Man*, 132.

67 Ibid., 349.

68 Ibid., 298.

69 Ibid., 188.

70 Lewis, *The Art of Being Ruled*, 20.

71 Ibid., 24.

72 Stirner, 43.

73 Lewis, *The Art of Being Ruled*, 375.

74 Lewis, *Time and Western Man*, 306.

75 Ibid., 300.

76 Ibid., 239.

77 Ibid., 338.

78 Ibid., 342.

79 Ibid., 342.

80 Ibid., 98.

81 Ibid., 98.

82 Ibid., 90.

83 Lewis, *The Caliph's Design*, 76.

84 'Most, Malatesta, Stirner, Bakunin, Kropotkin, Elisée Reclus, Spencer, and Benjamin Tucker, whose *Instead of a Book* proclaimed the liberty of the non-invasive individual'. – James Joyce in a note to his biographer Herbert Gorman. Quoted in Richard Ellman, *James Joyce: A Biography* (Oxford: Oxford University Press, 1982), 142.

85 James Joyce, 'A Portrait of the Artist' [1904]. *Poems and Shorter Writings*, eds. Richard Ellmann, A. Walton Litz and John Whittier-Ferguson (London: Faber and Faber, 1991), 212.

86 James Joyce, *Ulysses* [1922], ed. Hans Walter Gabler (London: Bodley Head, 1986), 16: ll.1164–1665; Jean-Michel Rabaté, *James Joyce and the Politics of Egoism* (Cambridge: Cambridge University Press, 2001), 55.

87 Joyce, 'A Portrait …', 14.

88   Rabaté, 12.

89   Sigmund Freud, *The Interpretation of Dreams* [1899]. Translated by
         A.A. Brill (Hertfordshire: Wordsworth, 1997), 358.

90   Lewis, *The Childermass*, 183.

91   Ibid., 194.

92   Ibid., 170.

Chapter 4

1   Ayn Rand, *The Fountainhead* (1943) (London: Penguin Books, 2007), 156.

2   Ibid.

3   Rand, 'Introduction' (1968), *The Fountainhead*, xi and ix.

4   For an overview of the impact Rand has had up on politicians and
         economists in the years since her death, see Gary Weiss, *Ayn Rand Nation:
         The Hidden Struggle for America's Soul* (New York: St. Martin's Press, 2012).
         For Trump's interest in the novelist see his interview with Kirsten Powers,
         'Donald Trump's "Kinder, Gentler" Version', in *USA Today*, 11 April 2016.
         'Trump described himself as an Ayn Rand fan. He said of her novel *The
         Fountainhead*, "It relates to business (and) beauty (and) life and inner
         emotions. That book relates to . . . everything." He identified with Howard
         Roark, the novel's idealistic protagonist who designs skyscrapers and rages
         against the establishment.' – The interview is available online at: http://
         www.usatoday.com/story/opinion/2016/04/11/donald-trump-interview-
         elections-2016-ayn-rand-vp-pick-politics-column/82899566/

5   Jennifer Burns, *Goddess of the Market* (Oxford: Oxford University Press,
         2009), 179.

6   Rand, *Fountainhead*, 24–25.

7   Burns, 2.

8   Rand, 'To the Readers of the Fountainhead' (1945).

9   Ibid.

10   Chris Matthew Sciabarra, *Ayn Rand: The Russian Radical* (University Park,
         PA: Pennsylvania State University Press, 1995), 67.

11 Ibid., 9.

12 Sciabarra, 17.

13 Barbara Branden, *The Passion of Ayn Rand* (New York: Anchor, 1987), 42.

14 Anne C. Heller, *Ayn Rand and the World She Made* (New York: Anchor, 2010), 41.

15 Ayn Rand, *We the Living* (New York: Signet, 1996), 134.

16 B. Branden, 42.

17 Ibid.

18 Ayn Rand, *For the New Intellectual* (New York: Signet, 1961), 33.

19 Max Stirner, *The Ego & His Own*, Book II. Translated by Steven T. Byington (New York: Dover, 2005).

20 Rand, *For the New Intellectual*, 14.

21 Ibid.

22 Ibid., 15.

23 See Chapter 3.

24 Rand, *For the New Intellectual*, 15.

25 'The more instinct with life a living unit the more empowered it is to change its present World into a fuller and more definite World.' Marsden, *The Egoist*, 1 April 1915; 51. 'Human individuality is best regarded as a kind of artificial godhead ... no Absolute need be ashamed of the feelings or thoughts of what we call a great artist or a great poet.' – Wyndham Lewis, *Time and Western Man*, ed. Paul Edwards (Santa Rosa: Black Sparrow Press, 1993), 372–376.

26 Rand, *For the New Intellectual*, 26–27. Compare Marsden's assertion that to fulfil the potential of the human ego necessarily means being Scientist or Artist: 'If science is the knowledge gained by applying to non-vital phenomena, a method of accurate description as opposed to that of imaginative interpretation, art is the product of the same method applied to vital (and mainly humanly vital) phenomena.' – Marsden, *The New Freewoman*, 1 November 1913; 182.

27 While science has made tremendous advances over the past three centuries, 'because during this period it has trusted to the results of unprejudiced observation of the 'thing', art, on the other hand, remains

'in a position analogous to that in which science was, when astronomy was astrology, chemistry alchemy, and mathematics witchcraft ...' – Marsden, *The New Freewoman*, 1 November 1913; 182, 15 October 1913; 166.

28 Rand, *For the New Intellectual*, 29.

29 Having insisted that art is the civilized substitute for magic, Lewis accuses his contemporaries of wishing to lead us back by means of art, to the plane of magic, to Shamanism: to retransform both of them [i.e. artist *and* scientist] into the primitive magician from which they both equally sprang...' – Lewis, *TWM*, 188.

30 Nathaniel Branden, 'Counterfeit Individualism', *The Virtue of Selfishness: A New Concept of Egoism*, ed. Ayn Rand (New York: Signet, 1964), 158.

31 'It is in "our Unconscious" that we live in a state of common humanity. There are no individuals in the Unconscious because a man is only an individual when he is conscious.' – Lewis, *TWM*, 301.

32 Ayn Rand, 'The Objectivist Ethics' (1961), *The Virtue of Selfishness*, ed. Ayn Rand (New York: Signet, 1964 [1961]), 38.

33 Ibid., 15.

34 Ayn Rand, *Atlas Shrugged* (New York: Penguin, 2007), 722.

35 Alan Greenspan, 'The Assault on Integrity' (1963). Republished in *Capitalism: The Unknown Ideal* (New York: Signet, 1967), 130.

36 Ayn Rand, 'First Philosophic Journal' (1934), *Journals of Ayn Rand*, ed. David Harriman (New York: Plume, 1999), 66.

37 B. Branden, 45.

38 Heller, 42.

39 B. Branden, 45.

40 Ibid.

41 Ayn Rand, *We the Living* (London: Cassell, 1936), 41. This passage was removed from subsequent editions in line with her post-Nietzschean approach to egoism.

42 In the sense earlier defined: as a tradition of thought. Reading Stirner apart from this tradition may not leave one with the impression that the self-interest he advocates is rational.

43 Ayn Rand, Recorded Biographical Interviews, 1960–1961 (Ayn Rand Archives).

44 Thomas Garrigue Masaryk, *The Spirit of Russia*, Vol. II. Translated by Eden and Cedar Paul (London: George Allen and Unwin, 1919, 1955), 473

45 B. Branden, 45.

46 Masaryk, 53.

47 Ibid., 392.

48 Allan Antliff, *Anarchy and Art: From the Paris Commune to the Fall of the Berlin Wall* (Vancouver: Arsenal Pulp Press, 2007), 71.

49 Ibid.

50 Nina Gurianova, *The Aesthetics of Anarchy: Art and Ideology in the Early Russian Avant-Garde* (Berkeley: University of California Press, 2012), 57.

51 Ibid., 308.

52 Fedorov. Quoted in Gurianova, 309.

53 Gurianova, 57.

54 Ibid., 155.

55 Antliff, 73.

56 Ibid.

57 Aleksandr Rodchenko, 'Rodchenko's System', *Tenth State Exhibition*. Translated by John E. Bowlt, ed. *Russian Art of the Avant-Garde*, 149–151.

58 Heller, 48.

59 Biographical interviews (Ayn Rand Archives).

60 Heller, 48.

61 Ayn Rand, 'Questions and Answers on Anthem', *The Ayn Rand Column*, 2nd edn, ed. Peter Schwartz (New Milford, CT: Second Renaissance, 1998), 123.

62 B. Branden, 143.

63 Yevgeny Zamyatin, *We* (1924). Translated by Clarence Brown (New York: Penguin, 1993), 124.

64 Ayn Rand, *Anthem* (New York: Penguin, 1995), 21.

65 Shoshana Milgram, 'Anthem in Manuscript: Finding the Words', *Essays on Ayn Rand's Anthem*, ed. Robert Mayhew (New York: Lexington Books, 2005), 136.

66 Vladmir Mayakovsky, *Polnoe sobranie sochinenii* (Moscow: Khudozhestvennaja Literature, 1957), Vol. IV, 122. See Edward James Brown, *Mayakovsky: A Poet in the Revolution* (Princeton, New Jersey: Princeton University Press, 1973), 228.

67 N. Branden, 'Counterfeit Individualism', 159.

68 Milgram, 141.

69 Heller, 104.

70 Milgram, 145.

71 Fyodor Dostoevsky, *Notes from Underground and the Double*. Translated by Ronald Wilks (London: Penguin, 2009), 12.

72 Rand, *Atlas Shrugged*, 1058.

73 N. Branden, 'Counterfeit Individualisms', 160.

74 Murray Rothbard to Richard Cornuelle, 11 August 1954, Rothbard Papers.

75 Jean-Paul Sartre, *Being and Nothingness* (1943). Translated by Hazel E. Barnes (London: Routledge, 2003), 86.

76 Karl Marx and Frederick Engels, *The German Ideology* (1847). *Collected Works Vol. 5*. Translated by Clemens Dutt, W. Lough and C.P Magill (London: Lawrence and Wishart, 1976), 266

77 Ayn Rand, *Introduction to Objectivist Epistemology* (1969–1971), eds. Harry Binswager and Leonard Peikoff (New York: Meridian, 1979), 60–61.

78 Slavoj Žižek, 'The Lesbian Session', *Lacanian Ink 12*, Summer 1997.

79 Ibid.

80 Žižek, 'Who Is Responsible for the US Shutdown? The Same Idiots Responsible for the 2008 Meltdown'. *The Guardian*, Friday 11 October, 2013.

SELECT BIBLIOGRAPHY

Allan Antliff, *Anarchy and Art: From the Paris Commune to the Fall of the Berlin Wall* (Vancouver, BC: Arsenal Pulp Press, 2007)

Hugo Ball, *Flight Out of Time: A Dada Diary*. Ed. John Elderfield (Berkeley: University of California Press, 1996)

Carl Albrecht Bernoulli, *Franz Overbeck und Friedrich Nietzsche—eine Freundschaft* (Jena: Eugen Diederichs, 1908)

B. Black, *The Right to be Greedy: Theses on the Practical Necessity of Demanding Everything* (Port Townsend, WA: Loompanics Unlimited, 1971/1983)

Rachel Blau Du-Plessis, *Pink Guitar: Writing as Feminist Practice* (Tuscaloosa: University of Alabama Press, 2006)

André Breton, *Conversations: The Autobiography of Surrealism*. Trans. Mark Polizzotti (Boston: Marlowe and Co., 1995)

André Breton, *The Lost Steps*. Trans. Mark Polizotti (Lincoln: University of Nebraska Press, 1996)

Jennifer Burns, *Goddess of the Market* (Oxford: Oxford University Press, 2009)

Albert Camus, *The Rebel* [1951]. Trans. Anthony Bower (New York: Random House, 1956)

Bruce Clarke, *Dora Marsden and Early Modernism: Gender, Individualism, Science* (Michigan: University of Michigan Press, 1996)

Gilles Deleuze, *The Logic of Sense* [1969]. Trans. Mark Lester. Ed. Constantin V. Boundas (London and New York: Continuum, 2004)

Jacques Derrida, *Specters of Marx* [1993]. Trans. Peggy Kamuf (New York and London: Routledge, 2006)

Fyodor Dostoevsky, *Notes from Underground and the Double*. Trans. Ronald Wilks. (London: Penguin, 2009)

Marcel Duchamp, eds. Anne d'Harnoncourt and Kynaston L. McShine (New York: Museum of Modern Art, 1984)

Marcel Duchamp, Works, Writing and Interviews, ed. Gloria Moure (Barcelona: Ediciones Polígrafa, 1984

Marcel Duchamp, The Writings of Marcel Duchamp, eds. Michel Sanouillet and Elmer Peterson (New York: De Capo Press, 1973)

Paul Edwards, *Wyndham Lewis: Painter and Writer* (New Haven: Yale University Press, 2000)

T.S. Eliot, *Collected Poems 1909–1962* (London: Faber and Faber, 1963)

T.S. Eliot, *Knowledge and Experience: In The Philosophy of FH Bradley* (New York: Farrar, Strauss and Company, 1964)

T.S. Eliot, *The Sacred Wood* (London: Methuen and Co., 1920, 1960)

T.S. Eliot, *The Use of Poetry and the Use of Criticism* [1933] (London: Faber and Faber, 1964)

Richard Ellman, *James Joyce: A Biography* (Oxford: Oxford University Press, 1982)

Sigmund Freud, *The Interpretation of Dreams* [1899]. Trans. A.A. Brill (Hertfordshire: Wordsworth, 1997)

Leslie Garner, *A Brave and Beautiful Spirit: Dora Marsden, 1882–1960* (Aldershot: Avebury, 1990)

Gerald F. Gaus and Fred D'Agostino, *Routledge Companion to Social and Political Philosophy* (London: Routledge, 2013)

Emma Goldman, *Anarchism and Other Essays* (New York: Mother Earth Publishing Association: 1910)

Robert Graham, *Anarchism: From Anarchy to Anarchism (300CE–1939), Vol. 1: A Documentary History of Libertarian Ideas* (Montreal: Black Rose Books, 2005)

Alan Greenspan, 'The Assault on Integrity' (1963). Republished in *Capitalism: The Unknown Ideal* (New York: Signet, 1967)

Nina Gurianova, *The Aesthetics of Anarchy: Art and Ideology in the Early Russian Avant-Garde* (Berkeley: University of California Press, 2012)

P. Hariharan, *Basics of Interferometry* (Amsterdam: Elsevier, 2007)

G.W.F. Hegel, *Lectures on the Philosophy of History* [1847]. Trans. J Sibree. Ed. CJ Friedrich (New York: Dover, 1956)

G.W.F. Hegel, *Lectures on the Philosophy of Religion* [1832]. Ed. Peter C. Hodgson (Oxford: Oxford University Press, 2006)

Anne C. Heller, *Ayn Rand and the World She Made* (New York: Anchor, 2010)

Glenn Hughes, *Imagism and the Imagists: A Study in Modern Poetry* (New York: Biblo and Tannen, 1960)

James Huneker, *Egoists: A Book of Supermen* (New York: C. Scribner's Sons, 1921)

Frederic Jameson, *Postmodernism, or, The Cultural Logic of Late Capitalism* (London: Verso, 1991).

James Joyce, 'A Portrait of the Artist' [1904]. *Poems and Shorter Writings*, eds. Richard Ellmann, A. Walton Litz, and John Whittier-Ferguson (London: Faber and Faber, 1991)

James Joyce, *Ulysses* [1922]. Ed. Hans Walter Gabler (London: Bodley Head, 1986)

R.D. Laing, *The Divided Self* (London: Penguin 1965/1990)

Michael H. Levenson, *A Genealogy of Modernism* (Cambridge: Cambridge University Press, 1984)

Wyndham Lewis, *The Apes of God* [1930]. Ed. Paul Edwards (Santa Rosa: Black Sparrow Press, 1997)

Wyndham Lewis, *The Art of Being Ruled* [1926]. Ed. Reed Way Dasenbrock (Santa Rosa: Black Sparrow Press, 1989)

Wyndham Lewis, *BLAST* [1914]. Ed. Paul Edwards (Santa Rosa: Black Sparrow Press, 2002)

Wyndham Lewis, *The Caliph's Design* [1919]. Ed. Paul Edwards (Santa Rosa: Black Sparrow Press, 1986)

Wyndham Lewis, *The Childermass* (London: Jupiter Books, 1965)

Wyndham Lewis, *Collected Poems and Plays*. Ed. Alan Munton (Manchester: Carcenet, 1996)

Wyndham Lewis, *Rude Assignment* [1950]. Ed. Toby Foshay (Santa Rosa: Black Sparrow Press, 1984)

Wyndham Lewis, *Tarr* (London: Chatto and Windus, 1928)

Wyndham Lewis, *Time and Western Man* [1928]. Ed. Paul Edwards (Santa Rosa: Black Sparrow Press, 1993)

Wyndham Lewis, *The Wild Body* (London: Chatto and Windus, 1927)

R.S. Longhurst, *Geometrical and Physical Optics* (London: Longmans, 1968).

Jean Maitron, *Le Mouvement anarchiste en France* (Paris: François Maspero, 1975)

Dora Marsden, *The Definition of the Godhead* (London: Egoist Press, 1928)

Dora Marsden, *The Mysteries of Christianity* (London: Egoist Press, 1930)

Karl Marx, *Capital: A Critique of Political Economy, Vol. One*. Trans. Ben Fowkes (London: Penguin, 1976)

Karl Marx and Friedrich Engels, *The German Ideology* [1845–1847]: *Collected Works Vol. 5*. Trans. Clemens Dutt, W. Lough and C.P. Magill (London: Lawrence and Wishart, 1976)

Thomas Garrigue Masaryk, *The Spirit of Russia, Vol. II*. Trans. Eden and Cedar Paul. (London: George Allen and Unwin, 1919, 1955)

Karl Menger, *Principles of Economics*. Trans. James Dingwall and Bert F. Hoselitz (Sussex: Terre Libertas, 1976)

Shoshana Milgram, 'Anthem in Manuscript: Finding the Words', *Essays on Ayn Rand's Anthem*. Ed. Robert Mayhew (New York: Lexington Books, 2005)

A. David Moody, *Ezra Pound: Poet, Vol. I: The Young Genius 1885–1920* (Oxford: Oxford University Press, 2007)

Robert Motherwell (ed.), *The Dada Painters and Poets: An Anthology* (Cambridge, MA and London: Harvard University Press, 1951/1981)

Francis M. Naumann, 'Marcel Duchamp: A Reconciliation of Opposites', *The Definitively Unfinished Marcel Duchamp*. Ed. Thierry de Duve (Cambridge, MA: MIT Press, 1991)

Theresa Papanikolas, *Anarchism and the Advent of Paris Dada: Art and Criticism 1914–1924* (Farnham, Surrey: Ashgate, 2010)

Richard Parry, *The Bonnot Gang: The Story of the French Illegalists* (London: Rebel Press, 1987)

Francis Picabia, *Écrits Critiques* (Paris: Mémoire du livre, 2005)

Jean-Michel Rabaté, *James Joyce and the Politics of Egoism* (Cambridge: Cambridge University Press, 2001)

Ayn Rand, *Anthem* (London: Cassell, 1938/New York: Penguin, 1995)

Ayn Rand, *Atlas Shrugged* (London: Penguin, 1957/2007)

Ayn Rand, *For the New Intellectual* (New York: Signet, 1961)

Ayn Rand, *The Fountainhead* (London: Penguin Books, 1943/2007)

Ayn Rand, *Introduction to Objectivist Epistemology* [1969–1971]. Eds. Harry Binswager and Leonard Peikoff. (New York: Meridian, 1979)

Ayn Rand, *Journals of Ayn Rand*. Ed. David Harriman (New York: Plume, 1999)

Ayn Rand, *The Virtue of Selfishness* (New York: Signet, 1964)

Ayn Rand, *We the Living* (London: Cassell, 1936/New York: Signet, 1996)

Herbert Read, *The Tenth Muse* (London: Routledge and Kegan Paul, 1957)

Georges Ribemont-Dessaignes, *Manifestes Dada: Poèms, Articles Projets, 1915–1920*. Ed. Jean-Pierre Begot (Paris: Editions Champ Libre, 1974)

William Rubin, *Dada and Surrealist Art* (New York: Henry N. Adams, 1969)

Michel Sanouillet, *Dada à Paris* [1965]. English language edition: Trans. Sharmila Ganguly (Cambridge, MA: MIT Press, 2012)

Jean-Paul Sartre, *Being and Nothingness* [1943]. Trans. Hazel E. Barnes. (London: Routledge, 2003)

Chris Matthew Sciabarra, *Ayn Rand: The Russian Radical* (University Park, PA: Pennsylvania State University Press, 1995)

Max Stirner, *The Ego and His Own: The Case of the Individual Against Authority* [1844]. Trans. Steven T. Byington [1907]. Ed. James L. Martin [1963]. Facsimile reprint (New York: Dover, 2005).

Raoul Vaneigem, *The Revolution of Everyday Life* [1967]. Trans. David Nicholson-Smith (London: Rebel Press, 2006)

Gary Weiss, *Ayn Rand Nation: The Hidden Struggle for America's Soul* (New York: St. Martin's Press, 2012)

John F. Welsh, *Max Stirner's Dialectical Egoism: A New Interpretation* (New York: Lexington Books, 2010)

William Carlos Williams, *Spring and All* [1923]. Ed. C.D. Wright (New York: New Directions, 2011)

William Carlos Williams, *Paterson* (New York: New Directions, 1995)

Yevgeny Zamyatin, *We* [1924]. Trans. Clarence Brown (New York: Penguin, 1993)

INDEX